U.S. DECENNIAL LIFE TABLES FOR 1969-71

Volume I, Number 5

United States Life Tables by Causes of Death: 1969-71

There will be five reports in Volume I. Numbers 1, 2, and 3 are published, and Number 4 will be published shortly.

There are 51 reports in Volume II. These contain the State life tables for 1969-71, and they are published.

For sale by the Superintendent of Documents, U.S. Government Printing Office
Washington, D.C. 20402 - Price $1.30
Stock No. 017-022-00383-0

Volume I, Number 5

United States Life Tables by Causes of Death: 1969-71

DHEW Publication No. (HRA) 75-1150

U.S. DEPARTMENT OF
HEALTH, EDUCATION, AND WELFARE
Public Health Service
Health Resources Administration
National Center for Health Statistics
Rockville, Maryland 20852
May 1975

U.S. DECENNIAL LIFE TABLES FOR 1969-71

NATIONAL CENTER FOR HEALTH STATISTICS

DIVISION OF VITAL STATISTICS

CONTENTS

UNITED STATES LIFE TABLES
BY CAUSES OF DEATH: 1969-71

T. N. E. Greville, Ph.D., Actuarial Adviser, *Division of Vital Statistics*
Francisco Bayo, Deputy Chief Actuary, *Social Security Administration*
Richard S. Foster, Actuary, *Social Security Administration*

INTRODUCTION

The life tables in this report are based on the 1970 Census of Population and the deaths of the 3-year period 1969-71. Separate life tables are presented for each of the color-sex categories total population, white males, white females, males other than white, and females other than white.

This is the second time that official life tables by causes of death are being published; the first such tables to be published were for 1959-61. Similar calculations were made with respect to the 1939-41 and 1949-51 decennial life-table programs, but the results were given only limited distribution. A few of these earlier values are included in this report in the comparisons with the results for earlier periods. However, for some of the causes of death this is the first time that tables have been calculated.

Values shown in the tables for 1959-61 and 1969-71 are based on data for the United States, defined as the 50 States and the District of Columbia. Those for 1939-41 and 1949-51 exclude Alaska and Hawaii. The deaths for each 3-year period by age, color, sex, and cause of death were taken as compiled by the Division of Vital Statistics, National Center for Health Statistics, and its predecessor agencies. For 1969-71 the causes were classified according to the *Eighth Revision International Classification of Diseases, Adapted for Use in the United States,* (ICDA)[1] and combined into the groups and subgroups listed in table A. The reader should note that the ICDA includes external causes of death as well as diseases. The values for earlier periods shown in table C are based on the most nearly comparable groupings of causes of death as listed in the Fifth, Sixth, and Seventh Revisions.

In table A the numbers in parentheses are the ICDA codes for the causes included in each group. The results of computations for the 15 groupings of causes shown in italics are presented in the detailed tables (1-20). A few selected results of computations for the remaining 10 groups of causes (as well as the 15 shown in italics) appear in text tables B and D. For economy of language, each of the 25 groupings of causes of death listed in table A will frequently be referred to as a "cause" or "cause of death."

It will be noted that the causes listed in table A are not mutually exclusive; some are subclasses of others. For example, causes 4 and 5 are included in cause 3, and cause 11 is a subclass of cause 10, which in turn is a subclass of cause 8.

The values computed include $_nq_x^{(-i)}$, $\ell_x^{(-i)}$, $_nL_x^{(-i)}$, and $\mathring{e}_x^{(-i)}$ for an abridged life table eliminating cause i. Also shown are values for which no cause has been eliminated, i.e., abridged life tables in which all causes have been combined. These tables are given for comparison purposes. They correspond exactly to the life tables for the total United States that were published previously in this series[2] by single years of age. In addition, values are shown for $_nd_x^i$ from a multiple decrement abridged table and for the probability of eventually dying from a specified cause of death. Each of these functions is defined and explained in the subsequent sections. The last section of text describes the special methodology used in the computations.

Table A. Groupings of causes of death used in this report

1. Infective and parasitic diseases (000-136)
2. Tuberculosis, all forms (010-019)
3. *Malignant neoplasms, including neoplasms of lymphatic and hematopoietic tissues (140-209)*
4. *Malignant neoplasms of digestive organs and peritoneum (150-159)*
5. *Malignant neoplasms of respiratory system (160-163)*
6. *Diabetes mellitus (250)*
7. Major cardiovascular-renal diseases (390-458,580-584)
8. *Diseases of the heart (390-398,402,404,410-429)*
9. Active rheumatic fever and chronic rheumatic heart disease (390-398)
10. *Ischemic heart disease (410-413)*
11. *Acute myocardial infarction (410)*
12. *Cerebrovascular diseases (430-438)*
13. *Arteriosclerosis (440)*
14. Nephritis and nephrosis (580-584)
15. *Diseases of the respiratory system (460-519)*
16. *Influenza and pneumonia (470-474,480-486)*
17. *Bronchitis, emphysema, and asthma (490-493)*
18. Peptic ulcer (531-533)
19. *Cirrhosis of the liver (571)*
20. Congenital anomalies (740-759)
21. *Certain causes of mortality in early infancy (760-778 except 769.3 and 773)*
22. *Motor vehicle accidents (E810-E823)*
23. *All other accidents (E800-E807,E825-E949)*
24. Suicide (E950-E959)
25. Homicide (E960-E978)

NOTE: Numbers in parentheses are Eighth Revision ICDA codes.

ABRIDGED LIFE TABLES

Tables 1-5 contain, in the first panel of each table under the heading "Eliminating no cause," the abridged life tables already referred to based on the total mortality rates for all causes combined. These abridged life tables contain only the funtions $_nq_x$, ℓ_x, $_nL_x$, and $\mathring{e}_x$, and the values are given by 5-year age groups only. Because of the significantly different mortality pattern under 1 year of age, the age group 0-5 is subdivided into the two groups 0-1 and 1-5. Except for this condensation, the values contained in these abridged tables are identical to those previously published in the complete life tables,[2] and they are included here primarily to permit quick comparison with the abridged life tables eliminating specified causes of death that appear in the remaining panels of tables 1-5. The latter tables were prepared on the assumption that the specified disease or condition was completely eliminated as a cause of death (but not as a disease or injury), i.e., under the assumption that there were no deaths from the eliminated cause, while the force of mortality at every age from other causes was that deduced from the mortality experience of 1969-71. This point is more fully discussed later. Each of these tables when compared with the corresponding life table for all causes of death combined would provide an indication of the effect on mortality of full control of the specified disease or other cause of death.

Explanation of Columns

The abridged life-table columns in tables 1-5 have the usual significance.

Period of life between two exact ages stated in years (x to x+n)—The age interval shown is the interval between two exact ages indicated. For instance, "20-25" means the 5-year interval between the 20th birthday and the 25th.

Proportion of persons alive at beginning of age interval dying during the interval ($_nq_x$)—This column shows the proportion of the members of the life-table cohort alive at the beginning of the indicated age interval who will die before reaching the end of that age interval. For example, in the first panel of table 3 in the age interval 20-25, the proportion dying is 0.00327—out of every 100,000 white females reaching their 20th birthday, 327 will die before reaching their 25th birthday. In other words, the $_nq_x$ values represent the probabilities that persons who are alive at the beginning of a specified age interval will die before reaching the beginning of the next age interval.

Number living at beginning of age interval (ℓ_x)—This column shows the number of persons, starting with a cohort of 100,000 live births, who will survive to the exact age marking the beginning of the indicated age interval. Thus the first panel of table 3 shows that out of 100,000 white female babies born alive, 98,468 will complete the first year of life and enter the second, 97,618 will reach age 20, and 30,490 will live to age 85.

Stationary population in the age interval, ($_nL_x$)—Suppose that a group of 100,000 persons like that assumed in the preceding column is born every year and that the proportions dying in each such group in each age interval throughout the lives of the members are exactly those shown in the $_nq_x$ column. If there were no migration and if the births were evenly distributed over the year, the survivors of these births would constitute what is called a stationary population—stationary because in such a population the number of persons living in any given age interval would never change. When an individual left an age interval, whether by death or by growing older and entering the next higher age interval, his place would immediately be taken by someone entering from the next lower age interval. Thus a census taken at any time in such a stationary community would always show the same total population and the same numerical distribution of that population among the various age intervals. In such a stationary population supported by 100,000 annual births, the ℓ_x column shows the number of persons who, each year, will reach the birthday that marks the beginning of the indicated age interval.

The $_nL_x$ column shows the number of persons in the stationary population in the indicated age interval on any given date. For example, the figure shown for white females in the age interval 20-25 in the first panel of table 3 is 487,300. This means that in a stationary population of white females supported by 100,000 annual births, and with proportions dying in each age interval always in accordance with the $_nq_x$ column, a census taken on any date would show 487,300 persons between exact ages 20 and 25.

Average number of years of life remaining at beginning of age interval ($\mathring{e}_x$)—The average remaining lifetime (also called expectation of life) at any given age is the average number of years remaining to be lived by those surviving to that age on the basis of a given set of age-specific rates of dying. In order to relate these figures to the preceding columns of the life table it is necessary to observe that the $_nL_x$ values of the life table can also be interpreted in terms of a single life-table cohort without introducing the concept of the stationary population. From this point of view, each $_nL_x$ represents the total time (in years) lived between two indicated birthdays by all those reaching the earlier birthday among the survivors of a cohort of 100,000 live births. Thus in the first panel of table 3 the figure

487,300 for white females in the age interval 20-25 is the total number of years lived between the 20th and 25th birthdays by the 97,618 who reached the 20th birthday out of 100,000 white females born alive. This $_nL_x$ value added to the corresponding values for all subsequent age intervals represents the total number of years lived after attaining age 20 by the 97,618 reaching that age. This total number of years divided by the number of persons reaching the starting age of 20 gives a quotient of 57.24 years, which is the average remaining lifetime of white females at age 20.

Eliminating Specified Causes of Death

Similar interpretations apply to the remaining panels of tables 1-5. However, in their case, a specified cause of death is being eliminated, i.e., in the preparation of the table it was assumed that deaths from the specified cause were impossible. In the text of this report a superscript *-i* in parentheses is used to denote life table functions based on the elimination of the ith cause of death. For example, $\ell_x^{(-i)}$ will denote the number of persons surviving to age x in the life table that eliminates the ith cause of death. In the actual tables the superscripts are not used, because there is no possibility of ambiguity. For example, in the second panel of table 3 the $_nq_x$ value of 0.00293 for white females at ages 20-25 represents the probability that a white female of exact age 20 will die before her 25th birthday if it is assumed that death from malignant neoplasms is impossible. This compares with the corresponding value of 0.00327 in the first panel, where all causes of death are assumed to be operative.

As a further example, consider the probability that a white female of exact age 15 will survive to age 45 (1) if all causes of death are operative and (2) if deaths from motor-vehicle accidents are eliminated. On the first assumption, the probability is $\ell_{45} \div \ell_{15}$ from the first panel of table 3, which gives $94,649 \div 97,902 = 0.96677$. On the second assumption, $\ell_{45} \div \ell_{15}$ in the next to last panel of table 3 gives $95,218 \div 98,020 = 0.97141$. It is perhaps more instructive to compare the complementary probabilities, obtained by subtracting these results from 1, that is, the probabilities that a white female of exact age 15 will not survive to age 45. This is 0.03323 if all causes of death are operating, but is reduced to 0.02859 if deaths from motor-vehicle accidents are eliminated.

The expectation of life of white females, as shown in the first panel of table 3, is 75.49 years at birth and 29.11 years at age 50. However, the second panel shows that elimination of malignant neoplasms as a cause of death increases these values to 78.06 years at birth and 31.20 years at age 50. The gain in expectation of life due to the elimination of a specified cause (in the example cited 2.57 years at birth and 2.09 years at age 50) is thought to be of sufficient interest for a separate set of tables (tables 16-20) to be devoted to it.

The elimination of a specified cause of death in these tables should not be interpreted as implying the elimination of the corresponding disease or injury. It is only the death from the specified cause that is assumed not to occur. Thus, if tuberculosis were the eliminated cause, the table eliminating it would assume that tuberculosis as a disease would continue at the level prevailing in the 1969-71 period. However, every person who would otherwise die from tuberculosis is, for the purposes of the life-table calculations, assumed to return to a "normal (usual) state of health" as of the moment in which he would have died. Any interactions between diseases in accelerating the death of a person are implicitly assumed to continue intact, including those pertaining to the eliminated cause.

It could be argued that if calculations were made on the assumption that the specified diseases or conditions themselves were eliminated, the resulting mortality rates would then be lower than those in these tables, since under that assumption the specified disease or condition could not contribute toward earlier deaths from the other causes.

It should be carefully noted that the tables in this report provide no guidance as regards the mortality among persons known to have a given disease or morbid condition, for example, mortality among persons with malignant neoplasms. Such information could be derived only from special studies of such groups of persons.

LIFE-TABLE DEATHS
FROM SPECIFIED CAUSES

An abridged life table for all causes combined usually includes an $_n d_x$ column, showing the number of deaths between exact ages x and $x+n$. These are generally referred to as "life-table deaths" because they represent the number of deaths that would be recorded among the survivors indicated by the life table if the mortality of the life table were applicable. The numbers of life-table deaths are different, both in absolute and relative terms, from the numbers of deaths observed in the population. In essence, they show the number of deaths that would be expected to occur between the two exact ages indicated in the cohort of 100,000 persons alive at birth that is assumed in the life table. They could be viewed as the expected distribution by age at death of the initial 100,000 persons.

For the purposes of this report it is of interest to have not only the distribution of the cohort by age at death but also the distribution by cause of death. This information is shown in tables 6-10 for five color-sex categories: total population, white males, white females, males other than white, females other than white. In these tables the initial group at age 0 was taken as 10,000,000 instead of the usual 100,000. The additional significant digits involved in this change are needed to improve the precision in the case of those causes that produce few life-table deaths.

To facilitate the calculation of some probabilities that may be based on these tables, a column of survivors, "Number living at beginning of age interval" is also provided. As an example of the computations that are possible, assume that one is interested in estimating the probability that a white female aged 20 will die before reaching her 25th birthday from injuries resulting from a motor vehicle accident. This can be calculated from table 8 as the ratio of 9,971, the number of life-table deaths at ages 20-25 due to motor vehicle accidents, to 9,761,800, the number of persons living at age 20. The probability is 0.00102, or about 102 deaths per 100,000 persons.

If one desired a similar probability, but for death occurring before the 35th birthday, the numerator of the ratio would be the sum of the life-table deaths at ages 20-25, 25-30, and 30-35, or 9,971+6,655+5,890. The denominator in this second example would be the same (9,761,800), since both probabilities relate to a white female aged 20, and the required probability is 0.00231.

It will be noted that the following general formula could be used to calculate the probability that a person aged x will die from the ith cause between ages y and $y+s$:

$$_{y-x}|_s q_x^i = {_s d_y^i}/\ell_x$$

where ℓ_x is the number of persons living at age x and $_s d_y^i$ is the number of life-table deaths from the ith cause occurring between ages y and $y+s$.

One special case of the above formula which is frequently calculated is the probability that a person aged x will eventually die from the ith cause. This probability is obtained by taking $y=x$

in the previous formula and at the same time allowing s to approach infinity. Calculations for this case have been made and are shown in tables 11-15 for the five color-sex categories previously mentioned.

It will be noted from table 13 that the probability that a white female aged 20 will eventually die from diabetes is 0.02497, while the probability that she will die from a disease of the heart is 0.43107.

A comparison is made in table B of the probabilities at birth of eventually dying from various causes. By this measure, major cardiovascular-renal diseases are the principal cause of death, and malignant neoplasms are the second most important cause. Care should be exercised in drawing conclusions from comparison of these probabilities by sex or color. It is possible for two groups of persons to experience identical death rates for one specified cause and yet have different probabilities of eventually dying from that cause. These probabilities depend sig-

Table B. Probability at birth of eventually dying from specified causes, by color and sex: United States, 1969-71.

Cause of death[1]	Total	White		All other	
		Male	Female	Male	Female
1. Infective and parasitic diseases	0.00734	0.00690	0.00576	0.01660	0.01190
2. Tuberculosis, all forms	.00246	.00271	.00120	.00809	.00388
3. Malignant neoplasms	.16300	.16943	.15924	.15352	.13477
4. Malignant neoplasms of digestive organs	.04879	.04816	.05028	.04736	.04222
5. Malignant neoplasms of respiratory system	.03292	.05214	.01333	.04368	.01107
6. Diabetes	.02008	.01473	.02444	.01675	.03660
7. Major cardiovascular-renal diseases	.58802	.56463	.63217	.47171	.59287
8. Diseases of the heart	.41206	.42233	.42108	.31723	.37200
9. Rheumatic fever and rheumatic heart disease	.00701	.00629	.00831	.00456	.00553
10. Ischemic heart disease	.37528	.39075	.38194	.27035	.31777
11. Acute myocardial infarction	.18892	.22798	.16486	.12157	.11935
12. Cerebrovascular diseases	.12244	.09505	.15090	.10619	.15991
13. Arteriosclerosis	.02211	.01624	.03045	.01144	.01995
14. Nephritis and nephrosis	.00446	.00383	.00379	.00924	.00987
15. Diseases of the respiratory system	.05910	.06864	.04831	.06341	.04565
16. Influenza and pneumonia	.03425	.03205	.03500	.04042	.03455
17. Bronchitis, emphysema, and asthma	.01564	.02461	.00730	.01167	.00483
18. Peptic ulcer	.00448	.00558	.00351	.00425	.00243
19. Cirrhosis of the liver	.01339	.01659	.00905	.02055	.01313
20. Congenital anomalies	.00495	.00519	.00483	.00491	.00439
21. Certain diseases of early infancy	.01148	.01191	.00869	.01898	.01487
22. Motor vehicle accidents	.01991	.02750	.01185	.03176	.01056
23. All other accidents	.02643	.02987	.02143	.04261	.02158
24. Suicide	.00950	.01413	.00600	.00645	.00241
25. Homicide	.00625	.00497	.00169	.04527	.00940

[1]Corresponding ICDA codes appear in table A. In some instances terminology is more abbreviated here than in table A.

Table C. Probability at birth of eventually dying from specified causes, by color and sex: United States, 1939-41, 1949-51, 1959-61, 1969-71.

Cause of death	White			
	1939-41	1949-51	1959-61	1969-71
	Male			
Tuberculosis, all forms	0.03126	0.02010	0.00679	0.00271
All other infective and parasitic diseases	.03411	(1)	.00456	.00419
Malignant neoplasms	.10780	.13589	.15256	.16943
Diabetes	.01847	.01218	.01267	.01473
Major cardiovascular-renal diseases	.51016	.58516	.59370	.56463
Influenza and pneumonia	(1)	.02859	.03240	.03205
Cirrhosis of the liver	(1)	(1)	.01284	.01659
Diseases of early infancy	.02402	(1)	.01632	.01191
Motor vehicle accidents	.02836	.02487	.02372	.02750
All other accidents	.04485	.03877	.03053	.02987
Suicide	.01641	(1)	.01431	.01413
Homicide	(1)	(1)	.00266	.00497
	Female			
Tuberculosis, all forms	0.02117	0.00961	0.00270	0.00120
All other infective and parasitic diseases	.02857	(1)	.00360	.00456
Malignant neoplasms	.13542	.15452	.15457	.15924
Diabetes	.03693	.02427	.02261	.02444
Major cardiovascular-renal diseases	.53174	.61932	.64469	.63217
Influenza and pneumonia	(1)	.03041	.03391	.03500
Cirrhosis of the liver	(1)	(1)	.00703	.00905
Diseases of early infancy	.01808	(1)	.01192	.00869
Motor vehicle accidents	.00974	.00868	.00921	.01185
All other accidents	.03937	.03485	.02488	.02143
Suicide	.00524	(1)	.00452	.00600
Homicide	(1)	(1)	.00114	.00169

[1]Not available.

NOTE: Values for 1969-71 are based on groupings of Eighth Revision causes of death; values for other periods are based on the most nearly comparable groupings as listed in the Fifth, Sixth, and Seventh Revisions.

nificantly on the mortality level from the remaining causes of death. Thus they are an acceptable measure of the importance of each cause of death within a single group of persons, but they provide only a general guide with respect to comparison between different groups.

The previous observation applies also to comparisons of the same group of persons at different periods in time. Further, it should be noted that the definitions of causes of death, as well as their interpretation by individual physicians, may change with the passage of time.

A comparison is made in table C for four different time periods of the probability at birth of dying from various specified causes. While dif-

ferent Revisions of the International Classification of Diseases were in effect during the different time periods, the data utilized are as nearly comparable as possible. The values shown in the table were calculated at the time of preparation of the corresponding decennial life tables for the United States, but virtually the same methods were used in the calculations in all four periods.

The steadily increasing importance of malignant neoplasms as a cause of death and the diminishing importance of tuberculosis are evident from the table. Most of the other causes fail to show a consistent upward or downward trend for every color-sex category.

Table C. Probability at birth of eventually dying from specified causes, by color and sex: United States, 1939-41, 1949-51, 1959-61, 1969-71—Con.

Cause of death	All other			
	1939-41	1949-51	1959-61	1969-71
	Male			
Tuberculosis, all forms	0.07574	0.05247	0.01621	0.00809
All other infective and parasitic diseases	.08501	([1])	.01127	.00851
Malignant neoplasms	.04716	.09182	.13128	.15352
Diabetes	.00833	.00850	.01258	.01675
Major cardiovascular-renal diseases	.41031	.50495	.52072	.47171
Influenza and pneumonia	([1])	.04544	.04761	.04042
Cirrhosis of the liver	([1])	([1])	.01032	.02055
Diseases of early infancy	.03103	([1])	.02686	.01898
Motor vehicle accidents	.02362	.02506	.02495	.03176
All other accidents	.04226	.04294	.04024	.04261
Suicide	.00395	([1])	.00600	.00645
Homicide	([1])	([1])	.02522	.04527
	Female			
Tuberculosis, all forms	0.06258	0.03342	0.00793	0.00388
All other infective and parasitic diseases	.06613	([1])	.00811	.00802
Malignant neoplasms	.07573	.10757	.12375	.13477
Diabetes	.02000	.01916	.02707	.03660
Major cardiovascular-renal diseases	.46176	.57901	.61152	.59287
Influenza and pneumonia	([1])	.04403	.03980	.03455
Cirrhosis of the liver	([1])	([1])	.00699	.01313
Diseases of early infancy	.02489	([1])	.02140	.01487
Motor vehicle accidents	.00619	.00725	.00753	.01056
All other accidents	.02194	.02452	.02336	.02158
Suicide	.00111	([1])	.00164	.00241
Homicide	([1])	([1])	.00670	.00940

GAIN IN EXPECTATION OF LIFE

Another measure of the importance of the various causes of death is the gain in expectation of life that could be achieved if a specified cause of death were eliminated. As discussed previously, the assumption made in the calculations is that deaths resulting from the specified cause do not occur but not that the corresponding disease or condition is eliminated.

The gain in expectation of life at age x due to the elimination of the ith cause of death is defined as the number of additional years that a person aged x would expect to live on the average if the ith cause of death were eliminated. In essence, the gain in expectation of life represents the excess in life expectancy if the ith cause is eliminated over the life expectancy if no cause is eliminated. Specifically, the values of gain in expectation of life shown in tables 16-20 are calculated as the excess of the life expectancy values in the remaining panels of tables 1-5 over the corresponding values in the first panel. For example, according to table 18 a white female aged 50 would expect to add 5.29 years to her life expectancy if diseases of the heart were eliminated as a cause of death. This value is the difference between the life expectancy at age 50 indicated in the first panel of table 3, 29.11

years, and the corresponding life expectancy indicated in the sixth panel, 34.40 years.

In table D, the gains in expectation of life at birth are shown for all the 25 groups of causes for which calculations were made. It will be observed that the gains are not additive, that is, the sum of the gains from two or more causes is not equal to the gain from eliminating the combination of those causes. For example, the gain in expectation of life due to the elimination of all accidents is greater than the sum of the gains due to the elimination of motor vehicle accidents and all other accidents. This can be seen as follows: If two causes were being eliminated jointly, it would be possible, if desired, to make the calculations in two stages, first computing the gain with respect to one of the causes and then calculating the additional gain with respect to the second cause. However, in the calculations with respect to the additional gain from the second cause, it would be appropriate to assume that the first cause was already eliminated. This necessary assumption of prior elimination of the first cause increases the numerical value of the additional gain with respect to the second cause. This is because the number of survivors at each age in the life table is greater with the first cause eliminated than with all causes operating. A more extreme example of this effect is as follows. If a 26th group of causes of death consisting of "all other causes" were added, the gain from elimination of this latter group of causes would not be extremely large, much smaller, in fact, than the gain from elimination of major cardiovascular-renal diseases. The list of groups of causes of death would then embrace all causes, and the sum of all the gains from eliminating each group of causes would not be excessively large, certainly much less than 100 years. Yet it is clear that if all causes of death were eliminated, people would become immortal and the gain in expectation of life would be infinite.

Table D suggests that future increases in life expectancy, if any, will have to come mainly

Table D. Gain in expectation of life at birth due to elimination of specified causes of death, by color and sex: United States, 1969-71.

Cause of death[1]	Total	White		All other	
		Male	Female	Male	Female
1. Infective and parasitic diseases	.17	.13	.12	.37	.32
2. Tuberculosis, all forms	.04	.03	.02	.14	.08
3. Malignant neoplasms	2.47	2.31	2.57	2.33	2.41
4. Malignant neoplasms of digestive organs	.60	.55	.62	.64	.61
5. Malignant neoplasms of respiratory system ..	.50	.69	.22	.66	.20
6. Diabetes	.24	.17	.28	.24	.55
7. Major cardiovascular-renal diseases	11.76	10.46	11.98	10.39	15.29
8. Diseases of the heart	5.86	6.14	5.17	5.29	6.28
9. Rheumatic fever and rheumatic heart disease .	.12	.10	.14	.09	.12
10. Ischemic heart disease	5.06	5.45	4.40	4.17	4.89
11. Acute myocardial infarction	2.43	3.01	1.79	1.71	1.62
12. Cerebrovascular diseases	1.19	.86	1.36	1.36	2.16
13. Arteriosclerosis	.13	.09	.17	.09	.16
14. Nephritis and nephrosis	.07	.05	.05	.15	.17
15. Diseases of the respiratory system	.83	.86	.61	1.22	.96
16. Influenza and pneumonia	.47	.41	.40	.81	.70
17. Bronchitis, emphysema, and asthma	.20	.26	.10	.17	.10
18. Peptic ulcer	.06	.06	.04	.07	.04
19. Cirrhosis of the liver	.28	.30	.20	.46	.35
20. Congenital anomalies	.29	.30	.30	.26	.26
21. Certain diseases of early infancy	.82	.82	.66	1.19	1.05
22. Motor vehicle accidents	.70	.93	.41	.97	.37
23. All other accidents	.63	.76	.35	1.21	.54
24. Suicide	.26	.34	.18	.19	.08
25. Homicide	.23	.16	.06	1.46	.35

[1]Corresponding ICDA codes appear in table A. In some instances terminology is more abbreviated here than in table A.

from reduction in mortality from some of the cardiovascular-renal diseases, especially diseases of the heart, or from maligant neoplasms.

METHODOLOGY

The methods used to calculate the values presented in this report are very closely related to those used in the construction of the 1969-71 life tables for all causes combined and make use of data already available from the national tables, together with additional data on deaths classified by cause of death. All the values published here conform to the results of the national tables and embody the adjustments and procedures used in the preparation of those tables. The data on deaths by cause were used as recorded for the 3-year period 1969-71. As in the case of deaths for all causes, deaths for which age was not stated were distributed over the various age intervals in proportion to the numbers actually reported in the respective age intervals.

The methodology of the 1969-71 life tables has been described in another report of this series.[3] Only certain details that directly concern the calculation of the life-table values by cause of death will be referred to here.

The additional calculations required for the tables contained in this report divide themselves naturally into two parts: (1) subdivision of the life-table deaths $_n d_x$ into the various components $_n d_x^i$ pertaining to various causes of death, shown in the multiple-decrement tables of life-table deaths (tables 6-10), and (2) calculation of the life-tables eliminating specified causes of death (tables 1-5). These two phases of the calculations will be discussed separately.

Number of Life-Table Deaths by Cause

The numbers $_n d_x^i$ of life-table deaths for different causes were calculated by means of the approximation

$$_n d_x^i = {_n r_x^i} \, {_n d_x}$$

where $_n r_x^i$ denotes the proportion of the deaths recorded during the 3-year period 1969-71 in the age interval x to $x+n$ attributable to the ith

cause of death, $_n d_x$ is the number of deaths in the same age interval in the corresponding national life table, and $_n d_x^i$ is the desired estimate of the number of life-table deaths between ages x and $x+n$ due to the ith cause.

This formula was applied by single years of age under age 5 and by 5-year age intervals for ages 5 to 110. Since the data on recorded deaths by cause for ages 100 and over were not subdivided by age, the proportion of deaths due to the ith cause for the entire age group 100 years and over was used for both age intervals 100-105 and 105-110. The calculated $_n d_x^i$ values for ages 1, 2, 3, and 4 were combined into a single value for the age interval 1-5, and a similar combination of values was used for the interval 85 years and over.

The probability that an individual aged x will eventually die from the ith cause was calculated by the formula

$$_\infty q_x^i = \ell_x^i / \ell_x$$

where ℓ_x is the number of survivors to age x in the life table for all causes of death combined and ℓ_x^i is the aggregate number of life-table deaths due to the ith cause at all ages x and over, or, in other words, the sum of the $_n d_x^i$ values for all age intervals between age x and the end of the life table.

It may be noted that, since the $_n d_x^i$ values represent a distribution of the $_n d_x$ deaths by cause, the ℓ_x^i values represent a distribution of the ℓ_x survivors according to the causes of their eventual deaths.

Life Tables Eliminating Specified Causes of Death

The first step in the calculation of life tables eliminating specified causes of death was the calculation of probabilities of survival $_n p_x^{(-i)}$ (with the ith cause of death eliminated), where $n=1$ for $x=0, 1, 2, 3,$ and 4 and $n=5$ for $x=5, 10, \ldots, 105$. These were calculated by the exponential formula

$$_n p_x^{(-i)} = {_n p_x}^{1 - {_n r_x^i}}$$

(For a justification of this formula, see reference 4.) Here $_n p_x = \ell_{x+n} / \ell_x$ was calculated from the corresponding life table for all causes combined. Values of $\ell_x^{(-i)}$ (designated as ℓ_x in the actual tables) were calculated successively starting with $\ell_0^{(-i)} = 100{,}000$ by the formula

$$\ell_{x+n}^{(-i)} = {}_np_x^{(-i)}\,\ell_x^{(-i)}$$

for $x = 1, 2, 3, 4, 5, 10, \ldots, 105$. Of course, not all these ℓ_x values appear in the tables. The others were used in the calculation of ${}_nL_x^{(-i)}$ and $\overset{o}{e}_x^{(-i)}$ values.

The 5-year probabilities of death actually shown in tables 1-5 were then calculated by the formula

$${}_nq_x^{(-i)} = 1 - {}_np_x^{(-i)}$$

based on the age intervals used in the tables. Thus $n=4$ for $x=1$, and calculations were not made for ages 85 and over. This formula represents the probability that a person aged x will die within n years if the ith cause of death is eliminated. It should not be confused with the probability (in the multiple-decrement table for all causes) that a person aged x will die within n years from any cause except the ith cause of death which may be written as

$${}_nq_x^{-i} = \frac{\ell_x - \ell_{x+n} - {}_nd_x^i}{\ell_x}$$

The latter probability should be slightly less than the former, that is,

$${}_nq_x^{(-i)} \geq {}_nq_x^{-i}$$

For age 0 and for ages $5, 10, \ldots, 105$, the number of persons living in the stationary population in the age interval x to $x+n$ was estimated by the formula

$${}_nL_x^{(-i)} = (n - {}_nf_x)\,\ell_x^{(-i)} + {}_nf_x\,\ell_{x+n}^{(-i)}$$

with $n=1$ for $x=0$ and $n=5$ for $x=5, 10, \ldots, 105$. Here the quantities ${}_nf_x$ were computed from the life table for all causes combined by the formula

$${}_nf_x = \frac{n\ell_x - {}_nL_x}{\ell_x - \ell_{x+n}}$$

The sole assumption made in deriving this approximation is that the average number of years lived by those who die within the age interval concerned is the same in the life table eliminating the ith cause of death as in the life table for all causes combined. In fact, the average number of years referred to is $n - {}_nf_x$.

The stationary population for the age interval 1-4 was estimated by the formula

$${}_4L_1 = \frac{1}{2}\,\ell_1 + \ell_2 + \ell_3 + \ell_4 + \frac{1}{2}\,\ell_5$$

In the calculation of the expectations of life a value for $T_{110}^{(-i)}$, the stationary population at ages 110 and over, was needed. This was estimated by the formula

$$T_{110}^{(-i)} = \overset{o}{e}_{110}\,\ell_{110}^{(-i)} / (1 - {}_\infty r_{100}^i)$$

Values of $\overset{o}{e}_{110}$ by color and sex were given in table 7 of the report on methodology.[3] This formula would be exactly correct if the force of mortality were constant at ages 110 and over in the life table for all causes combined. Under the method of extrapolation used in the calculation of the national life tables,[3] the force of mortality is, in fact, approaching constancy by age 110.

A calculation was made to test this assumption in a particular rather extreme case. The preceding formula for $T_{110}^{(-i)}$ is equivalent to

$$\overset{o}{e}_{110}^{(-i)} = \overset{o}{e}_{110} / (1 - {}_\infty r_{100}^i)$$

In the case of females other than white with ${}_\infty r_{100}^i = 0.3$ (a particularly large value) this formula gives $\overset{o}{e}_{110}^{(-i)} = 12.80$. Using the method of extrapolation in the report on methodology[3] to calculate the values of $q_x^{(-i)}$ to age 145, assuming that the force of mortality is constant within each 1-year age interval, so that

$$L_x^{(-i)} = -d_x^{(-i)} / ln\,(1 - q_x^{(-i)})$$

for each age x from 110 to 145, and finally assuming that $q_x^{(-i)}$ has the constant value 0.079 at ages 146 and over, so that $\overset{o}{e}_{146}^{(-i)} = -1/ln\,(1 - .079) = 12.15$, gives 12.57 as the value of $\overset{o}{e}_{110}^{(-i)}$.

This may be considered the correct value. The error resulting from the use of the approximate formula is therefore 1.8 percent. The error in $\overset{\circ}{e}_{85}^{(-i)}$ (85 being the highest age shown in the tables) would be much smaller.

With the value of $T_{110}^{(-i)}$ available, values of $T_x^{(-i)}$ for successively younger ages were calculated by

$$T_x^{(-i)} = T_{x+n}^{(-i)} + {}_n L_x^{(-i)}$$

and finally the required values of $\overset{\circ}{e}_x^{(-i)}$ were obtained by

$$\overset{\circ}{e}_x^{(-i)} = T_x^{(-i)} / \ell_x^{(-i)}$$

The gain in expectation of life due to the elimination of a specified cause of death was taken as the difference between the expectation in the life table eliminating this cause of death and the expectation at the same age in the life table for all causes of death combined. If we denote the gain due to the elimination of the ith cause by $g_x^{(-i)}$, then

$$g_x^{(-i)} = \overset{\circ}{e}_x^{(-i)} - \overset{\circ}{e}_x$$

It should be pointed out that the accuracy of the estimated gain in expectation decreases as the gain itself increases. For example, the estimated gain from elimination of tuberculosis or of motor vehicle accidents may be regarded as reasonably accurate. However, the estimated gain from elimination of malignant neoplasms or of diseases of the heart should be regarded as less accurate.

This difference in the degree of accuracy is due principally to two factors. In general the accuracy of the approximations used in the calculations varies with the postulated change in the death rates. The larger the assumed change, the smaller the accuracy of the approximations. In addition, most of the large gains in expectation of life are possible only at the older ages, and, as will be observed from the methodology described in this report and in the report on methodology[3] for the life tables for all causes combined, the accuracy of the death rates and of the approximations used is less for the older ages than for the younger ages.

REFERENCES

[1] National Center for Health Statistics: *Eighth Revision International Classification of Diseases, Adapted for Use in the United States.* PHS Pub. No. 1693. Public Health Service. Washington. U.S. Government Printing Office, 1967.

[2] National Center for Health Statistics: United States life tables, 1969-71. *U.S. Decennial Life Tables for 1969-71*, Vol. 1, No. 1. DHEW Pub. No. (HRA) 75-1150. Health Resources Administration. Washington. U.S. Government Printing Office, May 1975.

[3] National Center for Health Statistics: Methodology of the national and State life tables for the United States, 1969-71. *U.S. Decennial Life Tables for 1969-71*, Vol. 1, No. 3. DHEW Pub. No. (HRA) 75-1150. Health Resources Administration. Washington. U.S. Government Printing Office, May 1975.

[4] Greville, T.N.E.: Mortality tables analyzed by cause of death. *The Record*, Vol. 37, No. 76. Chicago. American Institute of Actuaries, Oct. 1948. pp. 283-294.

LIST OF DETAILED TABLES

Table 1. ABRIDGED LIFE TABLES FOR ALL CAUSES OF DEATH COMBINED AND ELIMINATING SPECIFIED CAUSES OF DEATH, FOR THE TOTAL POPULATION: UNITED STATES, 1969-71

| Period of life between two exact ages stated in years | Proportion of persons alive at beginning of age interval dying during interval | Of 100,000 born alive | | Average number of years of life remaining at beginning of age interval | Proportion of persons alive at beginning of age interval dying during interval | Of 100,000 born alive | | Average number of years of life remaining at beginning of age interval |
| | | Number living at beginning of age interval | Stationary population in the age interval | | | Number living at beginning of age interval | Stationary population in the age interval | |
x to $x+n$	$_nq_x$	ℓ_x	$_nL_x$	$\overset{\circ}{e}_x$	$_nq_x$	ℓ_x	$_nL_x$	$\overset{\circ}{e}_x$
	ELIMINATING NO CAUSE				MALIGNANT NEOPLASMS			
0-1-------------	0.02002	100,000	98,283	70.75	0.01998	100,000	98,286	73.22
1-5-------------	.00337	97,998	391,225	71.19	.00307	98,002	391,296	73.71
5-10------------	.00213	97,668	487,781	67.43	.00179	97,701	488,035	69.94
10-15-----------	.00204	97,460	486,880	62.57	.00178	97,526	487,263	65.06
15-20-----------	.00560	97,261	485,069	57.69	.00525	97,352	485,601	60.17
20-25-----------	.00740	96,716	481,813	53.00	.00695	96,841	482,544	55.47
25-30-----------	.00722	96,000	478,267	48.37	.00658	96,168	479,257	50.84
30-35-----------	.00866	95,307	474,562	43.71	.00758	95,535	475,944	46.16
35-40-----------	.01228	94,482	469,696	39.07	.01028	94,811	471,774	41.49
40-45-----------	.01859	93,322	462,558	34.52	.01480	93,836	465,938	36.90
45-50-----------	.02855	91,587	451,806	30.12	.02182	92,448	457,513	32.41
50-55-----------	.04341	88,972	435,805	25.93	.03242	90,431	445,281	28.08
55-60-----------	.06557	85,110	412,350	21.99	.04877	87,499	427,400	23.93
60-65-----------	.09551	79,529	379,531	18.34	.07264	83,231	401,737	20.02
65-70-----------	.13831	71,933	335,762	15.00	.10847	77,185	365,811	16.38
70-75-----------	.19810	61,984	280,195	12.00	.16263	68,813	316,974	13.06
75-80-----------	.29011	49,705	212,979	9.32	.24935	57,622	252,692	10.10
80-85-----------	.40745	35,285	139,900	7.10	.36729	43,254	175,909	7.61
85 and over-----	1.00000	20,908	110,465	5.28	1.00000	27,367	153,114	5.59
	MALIGNANT NEOPLASMS OF DIGESTIVE ORGANS				MALIGNANT NEOPLASMS OF RESPIRATORY SYSTEM			
0-1-------------	0.02002	100,000	98,283	71.35	0.02002	100,000	98,283	71.25
1-5-------------	.00337	97,998	391,225	71.80	.00337	97,998	391,225	71.70
5-10------------	.00213	97,668	487,781	68.04	.00213	97,668	487,781	67.94
10-15-----------	.00204	97,460	486,880	63.18	.00204	97,460	486,880	63.08
15-20-----------	.00559	97,261	485,071	58.31	.00560	97,261	485,071	58.20
20-25-----------	.00737	96,717	481,825	53.62	.00739	96,717	481,820	53.51
25-30-----------	.00715	96,004	478,302	49.00	.00719	96,002	478,282	48.89
30-35-----------	.00851	95,317	474,645	44.33	.00857	95,311	474,601	44.23
35-40-----------	.01197	94,506	469,884	39.69	.01198	94,494	469,822	39.59
40-45-----------	.01793	93,375	462,965	35.14	.01779	93,362	462,931	35.04
45-50-----------	.02724	91,701	452,650	30.73	.02694	91,701	452,716	30.62
50-55-----------	.04096	89,203	437,450	26.52	.04054	89,231	437,674	26.40
55-60-----------	.06141	85,550	415,323	22.54	.06099	85,614	415,721	22.40
60-65-----------	.08939	80,296	384,363	18.84	.08935	80,393	384,836	18.68
65-70-----------	.12962	73,118	342,819	15.43	.13087	73,210	343,031	15.26
70-75-----------	.18688	63,640	289,409	12.34	.19060	63,629	288,788	12.17
75-80-----------	.27625	51,747	223,497	9.59	.28339	51,502	221,533	9.42
80-85-----------	.39289	37,452	149,876	7.28	.40266	36,907	146,780	7.15
85 and over-----	1.00000	22,737	122,738	5.40	1.00000	22,046	117,037	5.31

Table 1. ABRIDGED LIFE TABLES FOR ALL CAUSES OF DEATH COMBINED AND ELIMINATING SPECIFIED CAUSES OF DEATH, FOR THE TOTAL POPULATION: UNITED STATES, 1969-71—Con.

Period of life between two exact ages stated in years	Proportion of persons alive at beginning of age interval dying during interval	Of 100,000 born alive		Average number of years of life remaining at beginning of age interval	Proportion of persons alive at beginning of age interval dying during interval	Of 100,000 born alive		Average number of years of life remaining at beginning of age interval
		Number living at beginning of age interval	Stationary population in the age interval			Number living at beginning of age interval	Stationary population in the age interval	
x to $x+n$	$_nq_x$	ℓ_x	$_nL_x$	$\overset{\circ}{e}_x$	$_nq_x$	ℓ_x	$_nL_x$	$\overset{\circ}{e}_x$
	DIABETES				DISEASES OF THE HEART			
0-1-------------	0.02002	100,000	98,283	70.99	0.01989	100,000	98,294	76.61
1-5-------------	.00337	97,998	391,225	71.44	.00331	98,011	391,292	77.17
5-10------------	.00212	97,668	487,784	67.67	.00209	97,687	487,887	73.42
10-15-----------	.00203	97,461	486,887	62.81	.00199	97,483	487,006	68.57
15-20-----------	.00558	97,263	485,084	57.93	.00549	97,289	485,234	63.70
20-25-----------	.00736	96,720	481,845	53.24	.00721	96,755	482,052	59.03
25-30-----------	.00713	96,009	478,335	48.62	.00687	96,057	478,635	54.44
30-35-----------	.00851	95,325	474,685	43.95	.00785	95,397	475,194	49.80
35-40-----------	.01206	94,514	469,903	39.30	.01024	94,648	470,973	45.18
40-45-----------	.01829	93,374	462,881	34.75	.01414	93,679	465,303	40.62
45-50-----------	.02809	91,666	452,295	30.35	.02003	92,355	457,439	36.16
50-55-----------	.04262	89,091	436,552	26.15	.02851	90,505	446,473	31.84
55-60-----------	.06428	85,294	413,504	22.20	.04118	87,924	431,056	27.70
60-65-----------	.09341	79,812	381,282	18.54	.05777	84,303	409,902	23.78
65-70-----------	.13505	72,357	338,307	15.18	.08197	79,433	381,522	20.08
70-75-----------	.19347	62,585	283,614	12.15	.11560	72,922	344,203	16.64
75-80-----------	.28401	50,477	217,046	9.44	.17041	64,492	295,369	13.47
80-85-----------	.40074	36,141	143,911	7.18	.24300	53,502	234,481	10.72
85 and over-----	1.00000	21,658	115,544	5.33	1.00000	40,501	339,122	8.37
	ISCHEMIC HEART DISEASE				ACUTE MYOCARDIAL INFARCTION			
0-1-------------	0.02001	100,000	98,284	75.81	0.02002	100,000	98,283	73.18
1-5-------------	.00337	97,999	391,229	76.35	.00337	97,998	391,225	73.67
5-10------------	.00213	97,669	487,786	72.60	.00213	97,668	487,781	69.91
10-15-----------	.00204	97,461	486,885	67.75	.00204	97,460	486,880	65.06
15-20-----------	.00559	97,262	485,079	62.89	.00559	97,261	485,071	60.18
20-25-----------	.00735	96,719	481,840	58.22	.00737	96,717	481,825	55.51
25-30-----------	.00707	96,008	478,342	53.64	.00712	96,004	478,310	50.90
30-35-----------	.00816	95,329	474,787	49.00	.00831	95,320	474,706	46.25
35-40-----------	.01075	94,552	470,381	44.38	.01120	94,528	470,165	41.61
40-45-----------	.01495	93,535	464,410	39.84	.01597	93,470	463,866	37.05
45-50-----------	.02128	92,137	456,089	35.40	.02333	91,978	454,860	32.61
50-55-----------	.03035	90,176	444,463	31.11	.03419	89,832	441,957	28.33
55-60-----------	.04390	87,439	428,117	27.00	.05069	86,760	423,398	24.24
60-65-----------	.06154	83,601	405,736	23.12	.07318	82,362	397,438	20.39
65-70-----------	.08704	78,456	375,873	19.47	.10658	76,335	362,128	16.79
70-75-----------	.12238	71,627	336,917	16.07	.15570	68,199	315,289	13.49
75-80-----------	.18005	62,862	286,411	12.96	.23629	57,580	254,361	10.50
80-85-----------	.25700	51,544	224,066	10.24	.34711	43,974	181,092	7.96
85 and over-----	1.00000	38,297	303,922	7.94	1.00000	28,710	168,996	5.89

Table 1. ABRIDGED LIFE TABLES FOR ALL CAUSES OF DEATH COMBINED AND ELIMINATING SPECIFIED CAUSES OF DEATH, FOR THE TOTAL POPULATION: UNITED STATES, 1969-71—Con.

Period of life between two exact ages stated in years	Proportion of persons alive at beginning of age interval dying during interval	Of 100,000 born alive		Average number of years of life remaining at beginning of age interval	Proportion of persons alive at beginning of age interval dying during interval	Of 100,000 born alive		Average number of years of life remaining at beginning of age interval
		Number living at beginning of age interval	Stationary population in the age interval			Number living at beginning of age interval	Stationary population in the age interval	
x to $x+n$	$_nq_x$	ℓ_x	$_nL_x$	$\overset{\circ}{e}_x$	$_nq_x$	ℓ_x	$_nL_x$	$\overset{\circ}{e}_x$
	CEREBROVASCULAR DISEASES				ARTERIOSCLEROSIS			
0-1------------	0.01998	100,000	98,286	71.94	0.02002	100,000	98,283	70.88
1-5------------	.00333	98,002	391,249	72.40	.00337	97,998	391,225	71.33
5-10-----------	.00210	97,676	487,829	68.64	.00213	97,668	487,781	67.56
10-15----------	.00201	97,471	486,943	63.77	.00204	97,460	486,880	62.70
15-20----------	.00554	97,276	485,158	58.90	.00560	97,261	485,069	57.82
20-25----------	.00730	96,737	481,943	54.21	.00740	96,716	481,813	53.14
25-30----------	.00705	96,031	478,462	49.59	.00722	96,000	478,267	48.51
30-35----------	.00834	95,354	474,866	44.92	.00865	95,307	474,562	43.85
35-40----------	.01171	94,558	470,200	40.28	.01227	94,482	469,696	39.21
40-45----------	.01765	93,451	463,402	35.73	.01857	93,322	462,563	34.66
45-50----------	.02699	91,801	453,199	31.32	.02852	91,589	451,823	30.27
50-55----------	.04092	89,324	438,050	27.12	.04333	88,977	435,846	26.08
55-60----------	.06158	85,669	415,866	23.16	.06538	85,122	412,445	22.14
60-65----------	.08869	80,393	384,962	19.51	.09508	79,556	379,742	18.50
65-70----------	.12620	73,263	344,101	16.15	.13733	71,992	336,206	15.17
70-75----------	.17678	64,017	292,689	13.11	.19584	62,105	281,081	12.17
75-80----------	.25404	52,700	230,498	10.37	.28533	49,942	214,583	9.51
80-85----------	.35246	39,312	161,359	8.03	.39775	35,692	142,395	7.30
85 and over-----	1.00000	25,456	154,501	6.07	1.00000	21,496	117,989	5.49
	DISEASES OF RESPIRATORY SYSTEM				INFLUENZA AND PNEUMONIA			
0-1------------	0.01792	100,000	98,463	71.58	0.01830	100,000	98,431	71.22
1-5------------	.00291	98,208	392,182	71.88	.00307	98,170	391,991	71.55
5-10-----------	.00200	97,922	489,083	68.09	.00204	97,869	488,808	67.76
10-15----------	.00193	97,726	488,231	63.22	.00197	97,669	487,940	62.90
15-20----------	.00544	97,537	486,483	58.34	.00550	97,477	486,169	58.01
20-25----------	.00719	97,007	483,315	53.64	.00727	96,941	482,965	53.32
25-30----------	.00697	96,310	479,872	49.01	.00706	96,236	479,482	48.69
30-35----------	.00832	95,639	476,294	44.34	.00844	95,557	475,855	44.02
35-40----------	.01176	94,844	471,609	39.69	.01196	94,750	471,099	39.37
40-45----------	.01781	93,728	464,742	35.13	.01812	93,617	464,122	34.82
45-50----------	.02732	92,059	454,400	30.72	.02789	91,920	453,591	30.41
50-55----------	.04145	89,544	439,017	26.51	.04248	89,356	437,880	26.21
55-60----------	.06234	85,832	416,506	22.54	.06424	85,560	414,799	22.25
60-65----------	.09039	80,482	385,061	18.86	.09359	80,063	382,447	18.60
65-70----------	.13071	73,207	343,045	15.47	.13544	72,570	339,235	15.25
70-75----------	.18727	63,638	289,341	12.41	.19337	62,741	284,336	12.23
75-80----------	.27528	51,721	223,508	9.68	.28232	50,609	217,824	9.55
80-85----------	.38904	37,483	150,367	7.39	.39557	36,321	145,103	7.30
85 and over-----	1.00000	22,900	126,617	5.53	1.00000	21,953	120,218	5.48

Table 1. ABRIDGED LIFE TABLES FOR ALL CAUSES OF DEATH COMBINED AND ELIMINATING SPECIFIED CAUSES OF DEATH, FOR THE TOTAL POPULATION: UNITED STATES, 1969-71—Con.

Period of life between two exact ages stated in years	Proportion of persons alive at beginning of age interval dying during interval	Of 100,000 born alive		Average number of years of life remaining at beginning of age interval	Proportion of persons alive at beginning of age interval dying during interval	Of 100,000 born alive		Average number of years of life remaining at beginning of age interval
		Number living at beginning of age interval	Stationary population in the age interval			Number living at beginning of age interval	Stationary population in the age interval	
x to $x+n$	$_nq_x$	ℓ_x	$_nL_x$	$\overset{\circ}{e}_x$	$_nq_x$	ℓ_x	$_nL_x$	$\overset{\circ}{e}_x$
	BRONCHITIS, EMPHYSEMA, AND ASTHMA				CIRRHOSIS OF LIVER			
0-1------------	0.01998	100,000	98,286	70.95	0.02001	100,000	98,284	71.03
1-5------------	.00334	98,002	391,249	71.39	.00337	97,999	391,229	71.48
5-10-----------	.00212	97,675	487,819	67.62	.00212	97,669	487,789	67.71
10-15----------	.00203	97,468	486,924	62.76	.00204	97,462	486,892	62.85
15-20----------	.00558	97,271	485,124	57.88	.00559	97,264	485,089	57.98
20-25----------	.00738	96,728	481,880	53.19	.00737	96,721	481,845	53.29
25-30----------	.00719	96,015	478,350	48.57	.00710	96,008	478,335	48.66
30-35----------	.00861	95,325	474,662	43.90	.00832	95,326	474,731	43.99
35-40----------	.01219	94,504	469,825	39.26	.01158	94,532	470,098	39.34
40-45----------	.01843	93,352	462,743	34.71	.01741	93,437	463,385	34.77
45-50----------	.02823	91,632	452,097	30.31	.02690	91,810	453,261	30.34
50-55----------	.04277	89,045	436,294	26.12	.04138	89,340	438,032	26.10
55-60----------	.06434	85,236	413,209	22.17	.06330	85,643	415,393	22.12
60-65----------	.09339	79,752	380,999	18.51	.09326	80,222	383,270	18.43
65-70----------	.13512	72,304	338,047	15.15	.13633	72,741	339,881	15.06
70-75----------	.19395	62,534	283,311	12.11	.19663	62,825	284,221	12.03
75-80----------	.28550	50,406	216,555	9.40	.28896	50,472	216,410	9.34
80-85----------	.40339	36,015	143,166	7.14	.40661	35,888	142,369	7.10
85 and over-----	1.00000	21,487	114,127	5.31	1.00000	21,296	112,611	5.29
	MOTOR VEHICLE ACCIDENTS				ALL OTHER ACCIDENTS			
0-1------------	0.01992	100,000	98,292	71.45	0.01948	100,000	98,329	71.38
1-5------------	.00291	98,008	391,353	71.90	.00256	98,052	391,623	71.79
5-10-----------	.00159	97,723	488,198	68.10	.00167	97,801	488,567	67.97
10-15----------	.00156	97,568	487,519	63.21	.00152	97,638	487,878	63.08
15-20----------	.00337	97,416	486,336	58.30	.00459	97,490	486,434	58.17
20-25----------	.00480	97,088	484,290	53.49	.00630	97,042	483,702	53.43
25-30----------	.00550	96,622	481,780	48.73	.00621	96,431	480,657	48.75
30-35----------	.00728	96,090	478,776	43.99	.00763	95,832	477,412	44.04
35-40----------	.01103	95,390	474,489	39.29	.01118	95,101	473,016	39.36
40-45----------	.01740	94,338	467,858	34.70	.01741	94,037	466,362	34.78
45-50----------	.02737	92,697	457,536	30.27	.02730	92,400	456,089	30.35
50-55----------	.04218	90,159	441,878	26.05	.04200	89,878	440,539	26.12
55-60----------	.06431	86,356	418,646	22.08	.06403	86,103	417,476	22.15
60-65----------	.09424	80,803	385,856	18.41	.09375	80,590	384,934	18.49
65-70----------	.13697	73,188	341,857	15.06	.13635	73,035	341,250	15.13
70-75----------	.19663	63,164	285,754	12.03	.19563	63,077	285,512	12.11
75-80----------	.28855	50,744	217,627	9.35	.28647	50,737	217,856	9.42
80-85----------	.40611	36,102	143,263	7.11	.40189	36,202	144,048	7.19
85 and over-----	1.00000	21,441	113,439	5.29	1.00000	21,653	116,181	5.37

Table 2. ABRIDGED LIFE TABLES FOR ALL CAUSES OF DEATH COMBINED AND ELIMINATING SPECIFIED CAUSES OF DEATH, FOR WHITE MALES: UNITED STATES, 1969-71

Period of life between two exact ages stated in years	Proportion of persons alive at beginning of age interval dying during interval	Of 100,000 born alive		Average number of years of life remaining at beginning of age interval	Proportion of persons alive at beginning of age interval dying during interval	Of 100,000 born alive		Average number of years of life remaining at beginning of age interval
		Number living at beginning of age interval	Stationary population in the age interval			Number living at beginning of age interval	Stationary population in the age interval	
x to $x+n$	$_n q_x$	ℓ_x	$_n L_x$	$\overset{\circ}{e}_x$	$_n q_x$	ℓ_x	$_n L_x$	$\overset{\circ}{e}_x$
	ELIMINATING NO CAUSE				MALIGNANT NEOPLASMS			
0-1-----------	0.02006	100,000	98,252	67.94	0.02001	100,000	98,256	70.25
1-5-----------	.00330	97,994	391,240	68.33	.00296	97,999	391,320	70.68
5-10----------	.00235	97,671	487,745	64.55	.00195	97,709	488,038	66.89
10-15---------	.00239	97,441	486,735	59.69	.00209	97,518	487,178	62.02
15-20---------	.00749	97,208	484,399	54.83	.00705	97,314	485,024	57.14
20-25---------	.00991	96,480	480,020	50.22	.00932	96,628	480,899	52.53
25-30---------	.00846	95,524	475,553	45.70	.00775	95,728	476,742	48.00
30-35---------	.00922	94,716	471,472	41.07	.00823	94,986	473,042	43.35
35-40---------	.01292	93,843	466,395	36.43	.01124	94,204	468,556	38.69
40-45---------	.02058	92,631	458,745	31.87	.01740	93,145	461,974	34.10
45-50---------	.03345	90,725	446,572	27.48	.02755	91,524	451,759	29.66
50-55---------	.05347	87,690	427,547	23.34	.04278	89,002	436,158	25.42
55-60---------	.08472	83,001	398,442	19.51	.06648	85,195	412,634	21.44
60-65---------	.12671	75,969	356,831	16.07	.09960	79,531	378,715	17.78
65-70---------	.18397	66,343	302,111	13.02	.14679	71,609	332,547	14.45
70-75---------	.25516	54,138	236,680	10.38	.21039	61,097	273,839	11.50
75-80---------	.35807	40,324	165,221	8.06	.30709	48,243	203,868	8.88
80-85---------	.47742	25,885	97,233	6.18	.42807	33,428	129,863	6.72
85 and over-----	1.00000	13,527	62,635	4.63	1.00000	19,118	94,895	4.96
	MALIGNANT NEOPLASMS OF DIGESTIVE SYSTEM				MALIGNANT NEOPLASMS OF RESPIRATORY SYSTEM			
0-1-----------	0.02006	100,000	98,252	68.49	0.02006	100,000	98,252	68.63
1-5-----------	.00330	97,994	391,240	68.89	.00330	97,994	391,240	69.04
5-10----------	.00235	97,671	487,745	65.11	.00235	97,671	487,745	65.26
10-15---------	.00239	97,441	486,735	60.26	.00239	97,441	486,735	60.41
15-20---------	.00747	97,208	484,401	55.40	.00748	97,208	484,401	55.55
20-25---------	.00987	96,481	480,032	50.79	.00989	96,481	480,030	50.94
25-30---------	.00839	95,528	475,591	46.27	.00843	95,527	475,576	46.43
30-35---------	.00906	94,727	471,563	41.64	.00911	94,722	471,529	41.80
35-40---------	.01260	93,869	466,592	37.00	.01253	93,860	466,564	37.16
40-45---------	.01992	92,686	459,159	32.44	.01949	92,684	459,241	32.60
45-50---------	.03208	90,840	447,428	28.04	.03120	90,878	447,799	28.19
50-55---------	.05081	87,926	429,243	23.88	.04925	88,042	430,128	24.02
55-60---------	.08002	83,459	401,566	20.02	.07739	83,706	403,272	20.12
60-65---------	.11954	76,781	361,960	16.53	.11609	77,228	364,706	16.59
65-70---------	.17376	67,602	309,517	13.42	.17034	68,263	313,111	13.42
70-75---------	.24219	55,855	245,972	10.70	.24104	56,635	249,566	10.65
75-80---------	.34236	42,328	175,110	8.31	.34550	42,984	177,482	8.23
80-85---------	.46156	27,837	105,714	6.35	.46866	28,133	106,319	6.26
85 and over-----	1.00000	14,988	71,017	4.74	1.00000	14,948	69,802	4.67

Table 2. ABRIDGED LIFE TABLES FOR ALL CAUSES OF DEATH COMBINED AND ELIMINATING SPECIFIED CAUSES OF DEATH, FOR WHITE MALES: UNITED STATES, 1969-71—Con.

Period of life between two exact ages stated in years	Proportion of persons alive at beginning of age interval dying during interval	Of 100,000 born alive		Average number of years of life remaining at beginning of age interval	Proportion of persons alive at beginning of age interval dying during interval	Of 100,000 born alive		Average number of years of life remaining at beginning of age interval
		Number living at beginning of age interval	Stationary population in the age interval			Number living at beginning of age interval	Stationary population in the age interval	
x to $x+n$	$_n q_x$	ℓ_x	$_n L_x$	$\overset{\circ}{e}_x$	$_n q_x$	ℓ_x	$_n L_x$	$\overset{\circ}{e}_x$
	DIABETES				DISEASES OF THE HEART			
0-1-------------	0.02006	100,000	98,252	68.11	0.01995	100,000	98,262	74.08
1-5-------------	.00330	97,994	391,240	68.50	.00324	98,005	391,295	74.59
5-10------------	.00235	97,671	487,748	64.72	.00232	97,687	487,833	70.83
10-15-----------	.00238	97,442	486,742	59.87	.00235	97,460	486,838	65.99
15-20-----------	.00747	97,210	484,411	55.00	.00737	97,231	484,541	61.13
20-25-----------	.00987	96,483	480,045	50.39	.00972	96,515	480,240	56.57
25-30-----------	.00838	95,531	475,608	45.87	.00811	95,577	475,900	52.10
30-35-----------	.00906	94,731	471,583	41.24	.00829	94,801	472,107	47.50
35-40-----------	.01271	93,873	466,589	36.59	.01017	94,015	467,851	42.88
40-45-----------	.02028	92,680	459,050	32.03	.01410	93,059	462,259	38.29
45-50-----------	.03303	90,800	447,031	27.64	.02047	91,747	454,371	33.80
50-55-----------	.05278	87,801	428,230	23.49	.03066	89,869	442,937	29.45
55-60-----------	.08361	83,167	399,458	19.65	.04792	87,113	425,731	25.30
60-65-----------	.12491	76,214	358,309	16.20	.07173	82,938	400,467	21.44
65-70-----------	.18123	66,694	304,152	13.14	.10546	76,989	365,252	17.90
70-75-----------	.25135	54,607	239,242	10.48	.14856	68,870	319,161	14.70
75-80-----------	.35309	40,881	168,016	8.14	.21497	58,639	261,419	11.82
80-85-----------	.47193	26,446	99,718	6.24	.29473	46,034	194,829	9.38
85 and over-----	1.00000	13,965	65,210	4.67	1.00000	32,467	237,131	7.30
	ISCHEMIC HEART DISEASE				ACUTE MYOCARDIAL INFARCTION			
0-1-------------	0.02005	100,000	98,253	73.39	0.02005	100,000	98,253	70.95
1-5-------------	.00330	97,995	391,244	73.89	.00330	97,995	391,244	71.40
5-10------------	.00235	97,672	487,750	70.13	.00235	97,672	487,750	67.63
10-15-----------	.00239	97,442	486,740	65.29	.00239	97,442	486,740	62.79
15-20-----------	.00747	97,209	484,409	60.44	.00748	97,209	484,406	57.93
20-25-----------	.00985	96,483	480,047	55.87	.00987	96,482	480,040	53.35
25-30-----------	.00828	95,532	475,636	51.40	.00833	95,530	475,614	48.85
30-35-----------	.00854	94,741	471,749	46:81	.00870	94,734	471,680	44.24
35-40-----------	.01062	93,931	467,335	42.19	.01115	93,910	467,114	39.61
40-45-----------	.01487	92,934	461,472	37.62	.01618	92,863	460,840	35.03
45-50-----------	.02172	91,552	453,138	33.15	.02450	91,361	451,604	30.56
50-55-----------	.03264	89,563	441,018	28.82	.03786	89,123	437,770	26.26
55-60-----------	.05090	86,640	422,813	24.70	.06019	85,749	416,589	22.19
60-65-----------	.07593	82,230	396,222	20.89	.09149	80,588	385,313	18.44
65-70-----------	.11110	75,986	359,453	17.39	.13610	73,215	341,904	15.03
70-75-----------	.15592	67,544	311,793	14.24	.19592	63,250	285,741	11.99
75-80-----------	.22516	57,013	252,704	11.40	.28846	50,858	217,306	9.30
80-85-----------	.30898	44,176	185,322	9.00	.40474	36,187	142,783	7.06
85 and over-----	1.00000	30,526	212,128	6.95	1.00000	21,541	112,788	5.24

Period of life between two exact ages stated in years	Proportion of persons alive at beginning of age interval dying during interval	Of 100,000 born alive		Average number of years of life remaining at beginning of age interval	Proportion of persons alive at beginning of age interval dying during interval	Of 100,000 born alive		Average number of years of life remaining at beginning of age interval
		Number living at beginning of age interval	Stationary population in the age interval			Number living at beginning of age interval	Stationary population in the age interval	
x to $x+n$	$_nq_x$	ℓ_x	$_nL_x$	$\overset{\circ}{e}_x$	$_nq_x$	ℓ_x	$_nL_x$	$\overset{\circ}{e}_x$
	CEREBROVASCULAR DISEASES				ARTERIOSCLEROSIS			
0-1--------------	0.02002	100,000	98,255	68.80	0.02006	100,000	98,252	68.03
1-5-------------	.00324	97,998	391,267	69.21	.00330	97,994	391,240	68.42
5-10------------	.00233	97,680	487,798	65.43	.00235	97,671	487,745	64.65
10-15-----------	.00235	97,453	486,803	60.57	.00239	97,441	486,735	59.79
15-20-----------	.00742	97,224	484,493	55.71	.00749	97,208	484,399	54.93
20-25-----------	.00982	96,502	480,152	51.11	.00991	96,480	480,020	50.32
25-30-----------	.00833	95,555	475,739	46.59	.00846	95,524	475,553	45.80
30-35-----------	.00900	94,759	471,735	41.96	.00921	94,716	471,472	41.17
35-40-----------	.01252	93,906	466,794	37.32	.01291	93,843	466,395	36.53
40-45-----------	.01987	92,730	459,386	32.75	.02056	92,631	458,750	31.97
45-50-----------	.03219	90,887	447,638	28.36	.03341	90,727	446,591	27.59
50-55-----------	.05127	87,962	429,323	24.22	.05338	87,696	427,596	23.45
55-60-----------	.08085	83,452	401,368	20.38	.08449	83,015	398,554	19.62
60-65-----------	.11965	76,705	361,582	16.94	.12617	76,001	357,079	16.19
65-70-----------	.17130	67,527	309,579	13.89	.18285	66,412	302,606	13.15
70-75-----------	.23304	55,960	247,693	11.23	.25267	54,269	237,586	10.51
75-80-----------	.32167	42,919	179,792	8.87	.35301	40,557	166,694	8.21
80-85-----------	.42448	29,113	113,373	6.90	.46748	26,240	99,245	6.33
85 and over-----	1.00000	16,755	87,634	5.23	1.00000	13,973	66,967	4.79
	DISEASES OF RESPIRATORY SYSTEM				INFLUENZA AND PNEUMONIA			
0-1--------------	0.01822	100,000	98,412	68.80	0.01856	100,000	98,383	68.35
1-5-------------	.00289	98,178	392,079	69.07	.00303	98,144	391,908	68.64
5-10------------	.00223	97,894	488,892	65.27	.00227	97,847	488,644	64.85
10-15-----------	.00229	97,676	487,928	60.41	.00232	97,624	487,662	59.99
15-20-----------	.00733	97,452	485,651	55.54	.00739	97,397	485,364	55.12
20-25-----------	.00970	96,738	481,355	50.93	.00977	96,678	481,040	50.51
25-30-----------	.00325	95,800	476,976	46.40	.00832	95,734	476,631	45.99
30-35-----------	.00896	95,009	472,988	41.77	.00906	94,937	472,608	41.35
35-40-----------	.01251	94,157	468,044	37.12	.01266	94,077	467,614	36.71
40-45-----------	.01986	92,979	460,624	32.56	.02017	92,886	460,096	32.14
45-50-----------	.03217	91,133	448,851	28.17	.03280	91,013	448,128	27.75
50-55-----------	.05113	88,201	430,518	24.01	.05248	88,028	429,400	23.60
55-60-----------	.08034	83,691	402,617	20.16	.08316	83,409	400,706	19.76
60-65-----------	.11899	76,967	362,940	16.69	.12432	76,472	359,631	16.31
65-70-----------	.17134	67,809	310,782	13.60	.18032	66,965	305,536	13.25
70-75-----------	.23766	56,157	247,927	10.88	.24901	54,890	240,799	10.60
75-80-----------	.33511	42,811	177,890	8.48	.34820	41,222	169,928	8.28
80-85-----------	.45125	28,465	108,864	6.51	.46320	26,869	101,924	6.38
85 and over-----	1.00000	15,620	76,414	4.89	1.00000	14,423	69,417	4.81

Period of life between two exact ages stated in years	Proportion of persons alive at beginning of age interval dying during interval	Of 100,000 born alive		Average number of years of life remaining at beginning of age interval	Proportion of persons alive at beginning of age interval dying during interval	Of 100,000 born alive		Average number of years of life remaining at beginning of age interval
		Number living at beginning of age interval	Stationary population in the age interval			Number living at beginning of age interval	Stationary population in the age interval	
x to $x+n$	$_nq_x$	ℓ_x	$_nL_x$	$\overset{\circ}{e}_x$	$_nq_x$	ℓ_x	$_nL_x$	$\overset{\circ}{e}_x$
	BRONCHITIS, EMPHYSEMA, AND ASTHMA				CIRRHOSIS OF LIVER			
0-1	0.02002	100,000	98,255	68.20	0.02005	100,000	98,253	68.24
1-5	.00328	97,998	391,262	68.59	.00330	97,995	391,244	68.63
5-10	.00234	97,677	487,778	64.81	.00235	97,672	487,750	64.85
10-15	.00238	97,448	486,772	59.96	.00239	97,442	486,740	60.00
15-20	.00747	97,216	484,444	55.10	.00748	97,209	484,406	55.14
20-25	.00989	96,490	480,075	50.49	.00989	96,482	480,035	50.53
25-30	.00844	95,536	475,618	45.97	.00838	95,528	475,591	46.01
30-35	.00918	94,730	471,549	41.34	.00894	94,727	471,590	41.38
35-40	.01285	93,860	466,494	36.70	.01228	93,880	466,717	36.73
40-45	.02041	92,654	458,895	32.14	.01931	92,727	459,491	32.15
45-50	.03308	90,763	446,839	27.75	.03150	90,936	448,024	27.73
50-55	.05261	87,761	428,069	23.61	.05091	88,072	429,936	23.55
55-60	.08282	83,144	399,501	19.78	.08163	83,589	401,872	19.67
60-65	.12306	76,258	358,852	16.32	.12346	76,765	361,167	16.18
65-70	.17805	66,873	305,484	13.25	.18101	67,288	306,897	13.09
70-75	.24715	54,966	241,384	10.56	.25301	55,108	241,212	10.42
75-80	.34914	41,381	170,483	8.19	.35647	41,165	168,834	8.08
80-85	.46960	26,933	101,718	6.26	.47625	26,491	99,591	6.19
85 and over	1.00000	14,285	66,774	4.67	1.00000	13,875	64,328	4.64
	MOTOR VEHICLE ACCIDENTS				ALL OTHER ACCIDENTS			
0-1	0.01996	100,000	98,261	68.87	0.01956	100,000	98,296	68.70
1-5	.00281	98,004	391,375	69.27	.00245	98,044	391,624	69.07
5-10	.00174	97,729	488,194	65.46	.00180	97,804	488,553	65.23
10-15	.00177	97,559	487,448	60.57	.00167	97,628	487,811	60.35
15-20	.00404	97,387	486,047	55.68	.00593	97,465	486,022	55.44
20-25	.00561	96,993	483,608	50.89	.00815	96,887	482,468	50.76
25-30	.00580	96,448	480,810	46.16	.00694	96,097	478,779	46.16
30-35	.00721	95,889	477,776	41.42	.00770	95,430	475,375	41.46
35-40	.01114	95,198	473,521	36.70	.01132	94,695	470,981	36.76
40-45	.01893	94,137	466,562	32.08	.01888	93,623	464,024	32.15
45-50	.03183	92,355	454,943	27.65	.03167	91,855	452,515	27.72
50-55	.05183	89,415	436,298	23.47	.05152	88,946	434,073	23.54
55-60	.08303	84,780	407,321	19.61	.08251	84,363	405,419	19.67
60-65	.12504	77,741	365,464	16.15	.12424	77,402	364,020	16.20
65-70	.18221	68,020	310,038	13.08	.18135	67,786	309,113	13.13
70-75	.25325	55,626	243,448	10.42	.25213	55,493	243,017	10.47
75-80	.35594	41,539	170,424	8.09	.35409	41,501	170,461	8.15
80-85	.47542	26,754	100,635	6.20	.47191	26,806	101,077	6.25
85 and over	1.00000	14,034	65,139	4.64	1.00000	14,156	66,514	4.70

Table 3. ABRIDGED LIFE TABLES FOR ALL CAUSES OF DEATH COMBINED AND ELIMINATING SPECIFIED CAUSES OF DEATH, FOR WHITE FEMALES: UNITED STATES, 1969-71

Period of life between two exact ages stated in years	Proportion of persons alive at beginning of age interval dying during interval	Of 100,000 born alive — Number living at beginning of age interval	Of 100,000 born alive — Stationary population in the age interval	Average number of years of life remaining at beginning of age interval	Proportion of persons alive at beginning of age interval dying during interval	Of 100,000 born alive — Number living at beginning of age interval	Of 100,000 born alive — Stationary population in the age interval	Average number of years of life remaining at beginning of age interval
x to $x+n$	$_nq_x$	l_x	$_nL_x$	$\overset{\circ}{e}_x$	$_nq_x$	l_x	$_nL_x$	$\overset{\circ}{e}_x$
	ELIMINATING NO CAUSE				MALIGNANT NEOPLASMS			
0-1	0.01532	100,000	98,673	75.49	0.01527	100,000	98,677	78.06
1-5	.00269	98,468	393,257	75.66	.00242	98,473	393,326	78.26
5-10	.00164	98,203	490,580	71.86	.00134	98,235	490,818	74.45
10-15	.00143	98,042	489,892	66.97	.00120	98,103	490,249	69.55
15-20	.00290	97,902	488,845	62.07	.00263	97,986	489,326	64.63
20-25	.00327	97,618	487,300	57.24	.00293	97,728	487,932	59.79
25-30	.00364	97,299	485,636	52.42	.00308	97,442	486,482	54.96
30-35	.00486	96,945	483,618	47.60	.00377	97,142	484,850	50.12
35-40	.00738	96,474	480,721	42.82	.00528	96,776	482,697	45.30
40-45	.01162	95,762	476,229	38.12	.00763	96,265	479,623	40.53
45-50	.01823	94,649	469,207	33.54	.01133	95,531	475,120	35.82
50-55	.02734	92,924	458,653	29.11	.01694	94,448	468,483	31.20
55-60	.04046	90,383	443,277	24.85	.02597	92,848	458,543	26.69
60-65	.05935	86,726	421,492	20.79	.04119	90,436	443,395	22.33
65-70	.09167	81,579	390,351	16.93	.06876	86,711	419,568	18.18
70-75	.14590	74,101	345,079	13.37	.11859	80,749	381,224	14.32
75-80	.23871	63,290	280,243	10.21	.20597	71,173	320,732	10.89
80-85	.36719	48,182	196,968	7.59	.33361	56,513	235,737	8.04
85 and over	1.00000	30,490	168,790	5.54	1.00000	37,659	218,825	5.81
	MALIGNANT NEOPLASMS OF DIGESTIVE ORGANS				MALIGNANT NEOPLASMS OF RESPIRATORY SYSTEM			
0-1	0.01532	100,000	98,673	76.11	0.01532	100,000	98,673	75.71
1-5	.00269	98,468	393,256	76.29	.00269	98,468	393,256	75.89
5-10	.00164	98,203	490,580	72.49	.00164	98,203	490,580	72.09
10-15	.00142	98,042	489,892	67.61	.00143	98,042	489,892	67.20
15-20	.00289	97,902	488,847	62.70	.00290	97,902	488,845	62.30
20-25	.00324	97,619	487,310	57.87	.00326	97,618	487,302	57.47
25-30	.00359	97,302	485,663	53.05	.00362	97,300	485,643	52.65
30-35	.00474	96,953	483,686	48.24	.00480	96,947	483,640	47.83
35-40	.00713	96,494	480,877	43.45	.00720	96,481	480,795	43.05
40-45	.01107	95,806	476,570	38.74	.01122	95,786	476,439	38.34
45-50	.01719	94,745	469,912	34.15	.01741	94,712	469,702	33.75
50-55	.02541	93,116	460,024	29.70	.02601	93,064	459,635	29.30
55-60	.03723	90,750	445,771	25.40	.03869	90,643	444,931	25.01
60-65	.05463	87,372	425,604	21.28	.05738	87,136	423,889	20.91
65-70	.08465	82,599	396,591	17.36	.08955	82,136	393,422	17.02
70-75	.13643	75,607	353,776	13.72	.14379	74,780	348,610	13.43
75-80	.22635	65,292	291,041	10.47	.23657	64,027	283,835	10.25
80-85	.35348	50,513	208,218	7.77	.36531	48,880	200,051	7.61
85 and over	1.00000	32,658	184,463	5.65	1.00000	31,024	172,164	5.55

Table 3. ABRIDGED LIFE TABLES FOR ALL CAUSES OF DEATH COMBINED AND ELIMINATING SPECIFIED CAUSES OF DEATH, FOR WHITE FEMALES: UNITED STATES, 1969-71—Con.

Period of life between two exact ages stated in years	Proportion of persons alive at beginning of age interval dying during interval	Of 100,000 born alive		Average number of years of life remaining at beginning of age interval	Proportion of persons alive at beginning of age interval dying during interval	Of 100,000 born alive		Average number of years of life remaining at beginning of age interval
		Number living at beginning of age interval	Stationary population in the age interval			Number living at beginning of age interval	Stationary population in the age interval	
x to $x+n$	$_nq_x$	ℓ_x	$_nL_x$	$\overset{\circ}{e}_x$	$_nq_x$	ℓ_x	$_nL_x$	$\overset{\circ}{e}_x$
	DIABETES				DISEASES OF THE HEART			
0-1-------------	0.01532	100,000	98,673	75.77	0.01523	100,000	98,681	80.66
1-5-------------	.00269	98,468	393,256	75.95	.00264	98,477	393,303	80.91
5-10------------	.00163	98,203	490,583	72.15	.00160	98,217	490,661	77.12
10-15-----------	.00141	98,043	489,902	67.26	.00139	98,060	489,991	72.24
15-20-----------	.00288	97,905	488,865	62.35	.00283	97,924	488,971	67.34
20-25-----------	.00322	97,623	487,335	57.52	.00316	97,647	487,472	62.52
25-30-----------	.00356	97,308	485,700	52.70	.00346	97,339	485,877	57.71
30-35-----------	.00474	96,962	483,729	47.88	.00450	97,002	483,983	52.90
35-40-----------	.00723	96,502	480,893	43.10	.00663	96,565	481,343	48.13
40-45-----------	.01144	95,804	476,478	38.39	.01005	95,925	477,390	43.43
45-50-----------	.01790	94,708	469,572	33.80	.01510	94,961	471,448	38.84
50-55-----------	.02677	93,013	459,218	29.37	.02146	93,527	462,922	34.40
55-60-----------	.03942	90,523	444,185	25.11	.02946	91,520	451,232	30.10
60-65-----------	.05751	86,954	422,979	21.03	.03940	88,824	435,866	25.93
65-70-----------	.08852	81,954	392,749	17.15	.05632	85,324	415,345	21.88
70-75-----------	.14104	74,699	348,716	13.56	.08437	80,518	386,614	18.03
75-80-----------	.23192	64,163	285,152	10.35	.13634	73,725	344,537	14.45
80-85-----------	.35966	49,282	202,386	7.69	.21234	63,674	284,790	11.32
85 and over-----	1.00000	31,557	176,482	5.59	1.00000	50,154	435,978	8.69
	ISCHEMIC HEART DISEASE				ACUTE MYOCARDIAL INFARCTION			
0-1-------------	0.01532	100,000	98,673	79.89	0.01532	100,000	98,673	77.28
1-5-------------	.00269	98,468	393,256	80.13	.00269	98,468	393,256	77.48
5-10------------	.00164	98,203	490,580	76.34	.00164	98,203	490,580	73.68
10-15-----------	.00142	98,042	489,892	71.46	.00143	98,042	489,892	68.80
15-20-----------	.00289	97,902	488,847	66.56	.00290	97,902	488,845	63.89
20-25-----------	.00325	97,619	487,310	61.75	.00325	97,618	487,302	59.07
25-30-----------	.00358	97,302	485,663	56.94	.00360	97,300	485,651	54.26
30-35-----------	.00470	96,953	483,693	52.14	.00475	96,950	483,667	49.44
35-40-----------	.00695	96,497	480,933	47.37	.00708	96,489	480,863	44.67
40-45-----------	.01055	95,827	476,791	42.68	.01086	95,806	476,616	39.96
45-50-----------	.01595	94,816	470,541	38.11	.01662	94,765	470,138	35.37
50-55-----------	.02269	93,304	461,549	33.68	.02420	93,190	460,652	30.93
55-60-----------	.03133	91,187	449,187	29.40	.03437	90,934	447,289	26.63
60-65-----------	.04211	88,330	432,880	25.27	.04826	87,809	429,053	22.48
65-70-----------	.06004	84,611	411,137	21.26	.07259	83,572	403,629	18.49
70-75-----------	.08975	79,531	380,867	17.45	.11549	77,506	366,478	14.73
75-80-----------	.14492	72,393	336,823	13.91	.19503	68,555	310,733	11.31
80-85-----------	.22578	61,902	274,798	10.83	.31360	55,185	232,942	8.41
85 and over-----	1.00000	47,926	395,542	8.25	1.00000	37,879	231,345	6.11

Table 3. ABRIDGED LIFE TABLES FOR ALL CAUSES OF DEATH COMBINED AND ELIMINATING SPECIFIED CAUSES OF DEATH, FOR WHITE FEMALES: UNITED STATES, 1969-71—Con.

Period of life between two exact ages stated in years	Proportion of persons alive at beginning of age interval dying during interval	Of 100,000 born alive		Average number of years of life remaining at beginning of age interval	Proportion of persons alive at beginning of age interval dying during interval	Of 100,000 born alive		Average number of years of life remaining at beginning of age interval
		Number living at beginning of age interval	Stationary population in the age interval			Number living at beginning of age interval	Stationary population in the age interval	
x to $x+n$	$_nq_x$	ℓ_x	$_nL_x$	$\overset{\circ}{e}_x$	$_nq_x$	ℓ_x	$_nL_x$	$\overset{\circ}{e}_x$
CEREBROVASCULAR DISEASES					ARTERIOSCLEROSIS			
0-1-----------	0.01529	100,000	98,676	76.85	0.01532	100,000	98,673	75.66
1-5-----------	.00265	98,471	393,276	77.05	.00269	98,468	393,256	75.84
5-10----------	.00161	98,210	490,623	73.25	.00164	98,203	490,580	72.04
10-15---------	.00140	98,052	489,949	68.36	.00143	98,042	489,892	67.15
15-20---------	.00285	97,915	488,922	63.45	.00290	97,902	488,845	62.24
20-25---------	.00318	97,636	487,412	58.63	.00327	97,618	487,300	57.42
25-30---------	.00351	97,326	485,803	53.80	.00364	97,299	485,636	52.60
30-35---------	.00461	96,985	483,872	48.98	.00486	96,945	483,618	47.78
35-40---------	.00694	96,537	481,133	44.20	.00738	96,474	480,721	43.00
40-45---------	.01093	95,867	476,905	39.49	.01161	95,762	476,231	38.30
45-50---------	.01706	94,819	470,307	34.90	.01821	94,650	469,217	33.72
50-55---------	.02555	93,201	460,414	30.46	.02730	92,927	458,677	29.29
55-60---------	.03769	90,820	446,015	26.19	.04035	90,390	443,336	25.04
60-65---------	.05457	87,397	425,738	22.11	.05908	86,743	421,629	20.98
65-70---------	.08254	82,628	397,140	18.23	.09094	81,618	390,675	17.13
70-75---------	.12756	75,808	356,297	14.63	.14403	74,195	345,843	13.58
75-80---------	.20419	66,138	298,325	11.39	.23420	63,509	281,899	10.42
80-85---------	.31074	52,633	222,544	8.64	.35747	48,635	199,993	7.81
85 and over-----	1.00000	36,278	232,119	6.40	1.00000	31,249	180,038	5.76
DISEASES OF RESPIRATORY SYSTEM					INFLUENZA AND PNEUMONIA			
0-1-----------	0.01395	100,000	98,792	76.10	0.01421	100,000	98,769	75.89
1-5-----------	.00234	98,605	393,890	76.18	.00245	98,579	393,760	75.98
5-10----------	.00152	98,374	491,465	72.35	.00156	98,337	491,272	72.17
10-15---------	.00133	98,224	490,822	67.46	.00136	98,184	490,618	67.28
15-20---------	.00278	98,093	489,828	62.55	.00281	98,051	489,609	62.36
20-25---------	.00312	97,821	488,350	57.71	.00318	97,775	488,105	57.53
25-30---------	.00345	97,516	486,762	52.89	.00352	97,464	486,488	52.71
30-35---------	.00462	97,179	484,840	48.06	.00472	97,121	484,529	47.88
35-40---------	.00704	96,730	482,073	43.27	.00718	96,663	481,708	43.10
40-45---------	.01111	96,049	477,771	38.56	.01133	95,969	477,324	38.39
45-50---------	.01743	94,982	471,034	33.96	.01784	94,882	470,449	33.80
50-55---------	.02613	93,326	460,903	29.52	.02676	93,190	460,093	29.37
55-60---------	.03869	90,887	446,130	25.24	.03966	90,696	444,984	25.10
60-65---------	.05688	87,371	425,134	21.15	.05821	87,099	423,539	21.03
65-70---------	.08812	82,401	394,970	17.26	.08987	82,029	392,850	17.16
70-75---------	.14059	75,140	350,855	13.68	.14274	74,657	348,224	13.60
75-80---------	.23020	64,576	287,255	10.48	.23279	64,001	284,299	10.42
80-85---------	.35419	49,711	204,824	7.84	.35703	49,102	201,968	7.79
85 and over-----	1.00000	32,104	184,735	5.75	1.00000	31,571	180,637	5.72

Table 3. ABRIDGED LIFE TABLES FOR ALL CAUSES OF DEATH COMBINED AND ELIMINATING SPECIFIED CAUSES OF DEATH, FOR WHITE FEMALES: UNITED STATES, 1969-71—Con.

Period of life between two exact ages stated in years	Proportion of persons alive at beginning of age interval dying during interval	Of 100,000 born alive		Average number of years of life remaining at beginning of age interval	Proportion of persons alive at beginning of age interval dying during interval	Of 100,000 born alive		Average number of years of life remaining at beginning of age interval
		Number living at beginning of age interval	Stationary population in the age interval			Number living at beginning of age interval	Stationary population in the age interval	
x to $x+n$	$_nq_x$	ℓ_x	$_nL_x$	$\overset{o}{e}_x$	$_nq_x$	ℓ_x	$_nL_x$	$\overset{o}{e}_x$
	BRONCHITIS, EMPHYSEMA, AND ASTHMA				CIRRHOSIS OF LIVER			
0-1-------------	0.01529	100,000	98,676	75.59	0.01531	100,000	98,674	75.69
1-5-------------	.00267	98,471	393,274	75.77	.00269	98,469	393,260	75.86
5-10------------	.00163	98,208	490,608	71.96	.00163	98,204	490,588	72.06
10-15-----------	.00142	98,048	489,924	67.08	.00142	98,044	489,904	67.18
15-20-----------	.00289	97,909	488,882	62.17	.00289	97,905	488,865	62.27
20-25-----------	.00325	97,626	487,345	57.34	.00325	97,623	487,330	57.44
25-30-----------	.00361	97,309	485,693	52.52	.00359	97,306	485,683	52.62
30-35-----------	.00482	96,958	483,692	47.70	.00473	96,957	483,706	47.80
35-40-----------	.00732	96,491	480,820	42.92	.00703	96,498	480,920	43.01
40-45-----------	.01150	95,785	476,370	38.22	.01094	95,820	476,670	38.30
45-50-----------	.01800	94,683	469,426	33.63	.01718	94,772	470,049	33.69
50-55-----------	.02696	92,979	459,008	29.20	.02601	93,144	460,030	29.24
55-60-----------	.03985	90,472	443,845	24.93	.03903	90,721	445,241	24.95
60-65-----------	.05850	86,867	422,350	20.86	.05801	87,180	423,974	20.85
65-70-----------	.09059	81,785	391,543	16.99	.09048	82,123	393,181	16.97
70-75-----------	.14460	74,376	346,586	13.42	.14493	74,692	348,001	13.40
75-80-----------	.23726	63,621	281,929	10.24	.23788	63,867	282,924	10.22
80-85-----------	.36571	48,526	198,551	7.61	.36654	48,674	199,058	7.60
85 and over-----	1.00000	30,779	170,828	5.55	1.00000	30,833	170,798	5.54
	MOTOR VEHICLE ACCIDENTS				ALL OTHER ACCIDENTS			
0-1-------------	0.01522	100,000	98,682	75.90	0.01495	100,000	98,705	75.84
1-5-------------	.00231	98,478	393,373	76.07	.00216	98,505	393,528	75.99
5-10------------	.00126	98,251	490,920	72.25	.00138	98,292	491,093	72.15
10-15-----------	.00109	98,127	490,392	67.34	.00121	98,156	490,510	67.25
15-20-----------	.00167	98,020	489,718	62.41	.00264	98,037	489,579	62.32
20-25-----------	.00225	97,857	488,740	57.51	.00300	97,778	488,162	57.48
25-30-----------	.00296	97,637	487,484	52.63	.00336	97,484	486,624	52.65
30-35-----------	.00425	97,348	485,767	47.78	.00454	97,156	484,744	47.82
35-40-----------	.00677	96,934	483,148	42.97	.00702	96,715	482,002	43.02
40-45-----------	.01100	96,277	478,929	38.25	.01118	96,036	477,692	38.31
45-50-----------	.01759	95,218	472,169	33.64	.01769	94,963	470,882	33.71
50-55-----------	.02663	93,543	461,865	29.20	.02669	93,283	460,570	29.27
55-60-----------	.03971	91,052	446,719	24.92	.03971	90,794	445,455	25.00
60-65-----------	.05854	87,436	425,108	20.84	.05843	87,189	423,930	20.92
65-70-----------	.09074	82,317	394,062	16.98	.09049	82,094	393,041	17.06
70-75-----------	.14480	74,848	348,751	13.40	.14408	74,665	348,024	13.49
75-80-----------	.23760	64,010	283,601	10.23	.23542	63,907	283,479	10.32
80-85-----------	.36631	48,801	199,606	7.60	.36154	48,862	200,433	7.69
85 and over-----	1.00000	30,925	171,326	5.54	1.00000	31,196	175,443	5.62

Table 4. ABRIDGED LIFE TABLES FOR ALL CAUSES OF DEATH COMBINED AND ELIMINATING SPECIFIED CAUSES OF DEATH, FOR MALES OTHER THAN WHITE: UNITED STATES, 1969-71

Period of life between two exact ages stated in years	Proportion of persons alive at beginning of age interval dying during interval	Of 100,000 born alive		Average number of years of life remaining at beginning of age interval	Proportion of persons alive at beginning of age interval dying during interval	Of 100,000 born alive		Average number of years of life remaining at beginning of age interval
		Number living at beginning of age interval	Stationary population in the age interval			Number living at beginning of age interval	Stationary population in the age interval	
x to $x+n$	$_nq_x$	ℓ_x	$_nL_x$	$\overset{o}{e}_x$	$_nq_x$	ℓ_x	$_nL_x$	$\overset{o}{e}_x$
	ELIMINATING NO CAUSE				MALIGNANT NEOPLASMS			
0-1	0.03408	100,000	97,173	60.98	0.03405	100,000	97,175	63.31
1-5	.00574	96,592	385,058	62.13	.00551	96,595	385,113	64.53
5-10	.00335	96,038	479,315	58.48	.00307	96,063	479,513	60.88
10-15	.00346	95,716	477,908	53.67	.00321	95,768	478,217	56.06
15-20	.01145	95,385	474,569	48.84	.01105	95,461	475,029	51.23
20-25	.02149	94,293	466,664	44.37	.02102	94,406	467,329	46.77
25-30	.02342	92,267	455,969	40.29	.02279	92,422	456,878	42.72
30-35	.02784	90,106	444,465	36.20	.02674	90,315	445,737	38.66
35-40	.03675	87,597	430,294	32.16	.03449	87,900	432,258	34.65
40-45	.04995	84,378	411,788	28.29	.04486	84,869	415,221	30.79
45-50	.06755	80,163	387,813	24.64	.05765	81,062	394,090	27.12
50-55	.09285	74,748	357,028	21.24	.07583	76,389	367,995	23.62
55-60	.12406	67,808	318,583	18.14	.09884	70,596	336,013	20.34
60-65	.16481	59,396	272,979	15.35	.13166	63,619	297,558	17.29
65-70	.21332	49,607	221,853	12.87	.17296	55,243	252,574	14.53
70-75	.28792	39,025	166,950	10.68	.23965	45,688	200,985	12.04
75-80	.35230	27,789	113,584	8.99	.30084	34,739	146,622	10.05
80-85	.39936	17,999	71,045	7.57	.34998	24,288	99,031	8.33
85 and over	1.00000	10,811	65,252	6.04	1.00000	15,788	103,369	6.55
	MALIGNANT NEOPLASMS OF DIGESTIVE ORGANS				MALIGNANT NEOPLASMS OF RESPIRATORY SYSTEM			
0-1	0.03408	100,000	97,173	61.62	0.03408	100,000	97,173	61.64
1-5	.00574	96,592	385,058	62.79	.00574	96,592	385,058	62.81
5-10	.00335	96,038	479,315	59.14	.00335	96,038	479,315	59.16
10-15	.00345	95,716	477,910	54.33	.00345	95,716	477,910	54.35
15-20	.01143	95,386	474,578	49.51	.01144	95,386	474,576	49.53
20-25	.02141	94,296	466,696	45.05	.02147	94,295	466,676	45.07
25-30	.02329	92,277	456,049	40.98	.02337	92,270	455,994	41.00
30-35	.02754	90,128	444,640	36.89	.02767	90,113	444,539	36.93
35-40	.03620	87,646	430,649	32.87	.03602	87,620	430,560	32.90
40-45	.04858	84,473	412,529	29.00	.04796	84,464	412,611	29.03
45-50	.06466	80,369	389,366	25.35	.06357	80,413	389,791	25.37
50-55	.08794	75,172	359,943	21.92	.08600	75,301	360,910	21.91
55-60	.11635	68,562	323,411	18.79	.11463	68,825	324,940	18.73
60-65	.15437	60,585	279,995	15.92	.15387	60,936	281,692	15.82
65-70	.20087	51,233	230,703	13.36	.20134	51,560	232,115	13.24
70-75	.27255	40,942	176,728	11.09	.27641	41,179	177,354	10.93
75-80	.33642	29,783	122,961	9.31	.34234	29,797	122,559	9.16
80-85	.38397	19,764	78,813	7.80	.39185	19,596	77,736	7.67
85 and over	1.00000	12,175	75,390	6.19	1.00000	11,917	72,640	6.10

Period of life between two exact ages stated in years	Proportion of persons alive at beginning of age interval dying during interval	Of 100,000 born alive		Average number of years of life remaining at beginning of age interval	Proportion of persons alive at beginning of age interval dying during interval	Of 100,000 born alive		Average number of years of life remaining at beginning of age interval
		Number living at beginning of age interval	Stationary population in the age interval			Number living at beginning of age interval	Stationary population in the age interval	
x to $x+n$	$n q_x$	l_x	$n L_x$	$\overset{o}{e}_x$	$n q_x$	l_x	$n L_x$	$\overset{o}{e}_x$
DIABETES					DISEASES OF THE HEART			
0-1	0.03408	100,000	97,173	61.22	0.03382	100,000	97,195	66.27
1-5	.00574	96,592	385,058	62.37	.00560	96,618	385,196	67.59
5-10	.00335	96,038	479,315	58.72	.00329	96,077	479,526	63.96
10-15	.00345	95,716	477,910	53.91	.00335	95,761	478,153	59.16
15-20	.01142	95,386	474,580	49.09	.01120	95,440	474,894	54.35
20-25	.02142	94,297	466,701	44.63	.02090	94,371	467,182	49.93
25-30	.02323	92,278	456,069	40.54	.02226	92,399	456,887	45.94
30-35	.02758	90,135	444,666	36.45	.02531	90,342	446,184	41.93
35-40	.03616	87,649	430,671	32.41	.03120	88,056	433,714	37.95
40-45	.04918	84,479	412,437	28.53	.03926	85,308	418,511	34.09
45-50	.06653	80,324	388,788	24.87	.04973	81,958	400,003	30.38
50-55	.09113	74,980	358,446	21.45	.06519	77,882	377,184	26.83
55-60	.12183	68,147	320,546	18.35	.08413	72,805	349,130	23.52
60-65	.16147	59,845	275,533	15.54	.10910	66,680	315,563	20.45
65-70	.20926	50,182	224,928	13.04	.13896	59,405	276,600	17.64
70-75	.28282	39,681	170,263	10.82	.18697	51,150	231,770	15.08
75-80	.34655	28,458	116,742	9.10	.22968	41,587	183,191	12.97
80-85	.39430	18,596	73,650	7.65	.26141	32,035	138,098	11.12
85 and over	1.00000	11,264	68,580	6.09	1.00000	23,661	218,147	9.22
ISCHEMIC HEART DISEASE					ACUTE MYOCARDIAL INFARCTION			
0-1	0.03407	100,000	97,174	65.15	0.03407	100,000	97,174	62.69
1-5	.00574	96,593	385,062	66.44	.00574	96,593	385,062	63.89
5-10	.00335	96,039	479,323	62.82	.00335	96,039	479,320	60.25
10-15	.00345	95,718	477,920	58.02	.00345	95,717	477,915	55.44
15-20	.01141	95,388	474,590	53.21	.01142	95,387	474,583	50.63
20-25	.02131	94,299	466,732	48.79	.02138	94,297	466,708	46.18
25-30	.02290	92,289	456,198	44.80	.02310	92,281	456,113	42.13
30-35	.02629	90,176	445,149	40.79	.02692	90,150	444,883	38.07
35-40	.03296	87,805	432,111	36.82	.03464	87,723	431,356	34.05
40-45	.04177	84,911	416,054	32.98	.04527	84,685	414,236	30.18
45-50	.05320	81,364	396,426	29.31	.05974	80,851	392,658	26.48
50-55	.06985	77,035	372,217	25.81	.08044	76,021	365,380	23.00
55-60	.09053	71,654	342,494	22.55	.10690	69,906	331,357	19.79
60-65	.11718	65,167	307,113	19.54	.14152	62,433	290,503	16.85
65-70	.14939	57,531	266,389	16.80	.18374	53,598	243,624	14.20
70-75	.20083	48,936	220,036	14.30	.25105	43,750	191,207	11.83
75-80	.24531	39,108	170,687	12.27	.31054	32,766	137,472	9.96
80-85	.27909	29,514	125,854	10.48	.35621	22,591	91,740	8.37
85 and over	1.00000	21,277	183,430	8.62	1.00000	14,544	97,246	6.69

Period of life between two exact ages stated in years	Proportion of persons alive at beginning of age interval dying during interval	Of 100,000 born alive		Average number of years of life remaining at beginning of age interval	Proportion of persons alive at beginning of age interval dying during interval	Of 100,000 born alive		Average number of years of life remaining at beginning of age interval
		Number living at beginning of age interval	Stationary population in the age interval			Number living at beginning of age interval	Stationary population in the age interval	
x to $x+n$	$_nq_x$	ℓ_x	$_nL_x$	$\overset{o}{e}_x$	$_nq_x$	ℓ_x	$_nL_x$	$\overset{o}{e}_x$
CEREBROVASCULAR DISEASES					ARTERIOSCLEROSIS			
0-1-------------	0.03400	100,000	97,180	62.34	0.03408	100,000	97,173	61.07
1-5-------------	.00567	96,600	385,105	63.53	.00574	96,592	385,058	62.22
5-10------------	.00332	96,052	479,393	59.88	.00335	96,038	479,315	58.57
10-15-----------	.00340	95,733	478,003	55.08	.00346	95,716	477,908	53.76
15-20-----------	.01133	95,407	474,703	50.25	.01145	95,385	474,569	48.94
20-25-----------	.02129	94,326	466,872	45.80	.02149	94,293	466,664	44.47
25-30-----------	.02300	92,318	456,318	41.74	.02342	92,267	455,969	40.39
30-35-----------	.02699	90,195	445,089	37.66	.02784	90,106	444,465	36.30
35-40-----------	.03514	87,760	431,432	33.63	.03674	87,597	430,296	32.27
40-45-----------	.04698	84,676	413,846	29.76	.04990	84,379	411,805	28.40
45-50-----------	.06291	80,698	391,300	26.10	.06747	80,169	387,857	24.75
50-55-----------	.08542	75,621	362,549	22.68	.09261	74,760	357,129	21.35
55-60-----------	.11284	69,161	326,827	19.56	.12365	67,837	318,786	18.27
60-65-----------	.14860	61,357	284,429	16.72	.16393	59,449	273,349	15.48
65-70-----------	.18861	52,239	236,817	14.19	.21156	49,703	222,499	13.02
70-75-----------	.25377	42,386	184,959	11.90	.28468	39,188	167,966	10.84
75-80-----------	.30951	31,630	132,789	10.10	.34729	28,032	114,941	9.16
80-85-----------	.34904	21,840	89,103	8.55	.39180	18,297	72,585	7.74
85 and over-----	1.00000	14,217	97,564	6.86	1.00000	11,128	69,111	6.21
DISEASES OF RESPIRATORY SYSTEM					INFLUENZA AND PNEUMONIA			
0-1-------------	0.02924	100,000	97,574	62.20	0.03010	100,000	97,503	61.79
1-5-------------	.00474	97,076	387,254	63.07	.00501	96,990	386,839	62.70
5-10------------	.00316	96,616	482,248	59.36	.00324	96,504	481,669	59.01
10-15-----------	.00328	96,310	480,908	54.54	.00336	96,191	480,299	54.20
15-20-----------	.01107	95,994	477,679	49.71	.01123	95,868	477,016	49.37
20-25-----------	.02091	94,932	469,956	45.24	.02114	94,791	469,206	44.90
25-30-----------	.02260	92,947	459,518	41.15	.02288	92,787	458,663	40.81
30-35-----------	.02664	90,846	448,380	37.04	.02702	90,664	447,398	36.71
35-40-----------	.03471	88,426	434,797	32.98	.03537	88,214	433,616	32.65
40-45-----------	.04718	85,357	417,134	29.08	.04807	85,094	415,668	28.76
45-50-----------	.06364	81,330	394,222	25.39	.06502	81,004	392,373	25.08
50-55-----------	.08764	76,154	364,696	21.94	.08978	75,737	362,313	21.64
55-60-----------	.11701	69,479	327,624	18.79	.12029	68,938	324,522	18.52
60-65-----------	.15583	61,349	283,305	15.95	.15994	60,645	279,442	15.70
65-70-----------	.20226	51,789	233,028	13.42	.20722	50,945	228,605	13.20
70-75-----------	.27286	41,314	178,302	11.18	.27913	40,388	173,670	11.00
75-80-----------	.33337	30,041	124,261	9.44	.34061	29,114	119,883	9.29
80-85-----------	.37875	20,026	80,133	7.96	.38548	19,198	76,481	7.84
85 and over-----	1.00000	12,441	79,204	6.37	1.00000	11,798	74,045	6.28

Period of life between two exact ages stated in years	Proportion of persons alive at beginning of age interval dying during interval	Of 100,000 born alive		Average number of years of life remaining at beginning of age interval	Proportion of persons alive at beginning of age interval dying during interval	Of 100,000 born alive		Average number of years of life remaining at beginning of age interval
		Number living at beginning of age interval	Stationary population in the age interval			Number living at beginning of age interval	Stationary population in the age interval	
x to $x+n$	$_nq_x$	ℓ_x	$_nL_x$	$\overset{\circ}{e}_x$	$_nq_x$	ℓ_x	$_nL_x$	$\overset{\circ}{e}_x$
BRONCHITIS, EMPHYSEMA, AND ASTHMA					CIRRHOSIS OF LIVER			
0-1--------------	0.03400	100,000	97,180	61.15	0.03407	100,000	97,174	61.44
1-5--------------	.00565	96,600	385,111	62.30	.00573	96,593	385,066	62.60
5-10-------------	.00332	96,054	479,403	58.64	.00335	96,040	479,325	58.95
10-15------------	.00342	95,735	478,011	53.83	.00345	95,718	477,920	54.14
15-20------------	.01138	95,408	474,697	49.01	.01143	95,388	474,588	49.32
20-25------------	.02141	94,322	466,823	44.54	.02134	94,298	466,722	44.86
25-30------------	.02333	92,302	456,164	40.45	.02281	92,286	456,203	40.78
30-35------------	.02773	90,149	444,702	36.36	.02633	90,181	445,164	36.67
35-40------------	.03648	87,649	430,604	32.32	.03406	87,806	431,884	32.59
40-45------------	.04959	84,451	412,218	28.45	.04641	84,815	414,642	28.65
45-50------------	.06694	80,263	388,414	24.80	.06371	80,879	392,022	24.92
50-55------------	.09175	74,890	357,904	21.39	.08919	75,726	362,366	21.43
55-60------------	.12222	68,019	319,876	18.29	.12073	68,972	324,610	18.28
60-65------------	.16257	59,705	274,728	15.48	.16188	60,645	279,153	15.44
65-70------------	.21049	49,999	223,957	12.99	.21100	50,827	227,599	12.93
70-75------------	.28448	39,475	169,215	10.78	.28650	40,102	171,701	10.71
75-80------------	.34828	28,245	115,742	9.07	.35133	28,613	117,023	9.01
80-85------------	.39555	18,408	72,845	7.63	.39871	18,560	73,291	7.58
85 and over-----	1.00000	11,127	67,610	6.08	1.00000	11,160	67,420	6.04
MOTOR VEHICLE ACCIDENTS					ALL OTHER ACCIDENTS			
0-1--------------	0.03398	100,000	97,181	61.95	0.03301	100,000	97,262	62.19
1-5--------------	.00505	96,602	385,212	63.12	.00427	96,699	385,802	63.31
5-10-------------	.00237	96,114	479,950	59.44	.00237	96,286	480,810	59.57
10-15------------	.00283	95,886	478,880	54.57	.00221	96,058	479,860	54.71
15-20------------	.00916	95,615	476,185	49.72	.00879	95,846	477,411	49.82
20-25------------	.01718	94,739	469,837	45.15	.01813	95,003	470,932	45.24
25-30------------	.01988	93,111	460,959	40.90	.02030	93,280	461,699	41.02
30-35------------	.02466	91,260	450,859	36.68	.02469	91,387	451,479	36.82
35-40------------	.03391	89,009	437,834	32.54	.03340	89,130	438,537	32.69
40-45------------	.04718	85,991	420,232	28.59	.04628	86,153	421,209	28.73
45-50------------	.06479	81,934	396,925	24.87	.06395	82,166	398,215	25.00
50-55------------	.09010	76,626	366,505	21.42	.08886	76,912	368,103	21.53
55-60------------	.12126	69,722	328,048	18.28	.12041	70,078	329,870	18.37
60-65------------	.16217	61,267	281,974	15.45	.16086	61,640	283,890	15.54
65-70------------	.21091	51,331	229,869	12.95	.20953	51,725	231,810	13.03
70-75------------	.28580	40,505	173,497	10.73	.28353	40,887	175,365	10.81
75-80------------	.35010	28,929	118,408	9.03	.34776	29,294	120,081	9.10
80-85------------	.39748	18,801	74,304	7.60	.39434	19,107	75,670	7.67
85 and over-----	1.00000	11,328	68,514	6.05	1.00000	11,572	70,821	6.12

Table 5. ABRIDGED LIFE TABLES FOR ALL CAUSES OF DEATH COMBINED AND ELIMINATING SPECIFIED CAUSES OF DEATH, FOR FEMALES OTHER THAN WHITE: UNITED STATES, 1969-71

Period of life between two exact ages stated in years	Proportion of persons alive at beginning of age interval dying during interval	Of 100,000 born alive		Average number of years of life remaining at beginning of age interval	Proportion of persons alive at beginning of age interval dying during interval	Of 100,000 born alive		Average number of years of life remaining at beginning of age interval
		Number living at beginning of age interval	Stationary population in the age interval			Number living at beginning of age interval	Stationary population in the age interval	
x to $x+n$	$_nq_x$	ℓ_x	$_nL_x$	$\overset{o}{e}_x$	$_nq_x$	ℓ_x	$_nL_x$	$\overset{o}{e}_x$
	ELIMINATING NO CAUSE				MALIGNANT NEOPLASMS			
0-1--------------	0.02765	100,000	97,738	69.05	0.02762	100,000	97,740	71.46
1-5-------------	.00476	97,235	387,817	70.01	.00454	97,238	387,872	72.48
5-10------------	.00234	96,772	483,231	66.34	.00211	96,797	483,417	68.80
10-15-----------	.00200	96,546	482,300	61.49	.00179	96,593	482,580	63.95
15-20-----------	.00453	96,353	480,786	56.60	.00425	96,420	481,179	59.06
20-25--------	.00699	95,917	477,996	51.85	.00661	96,010	478,546	54.30
25-30--------	.00921	95,247	474,149	47.19	.00849	95,376	474,953	49.64
30-35-----------	.01321	94,370	468,935	42.61	.01173	94,566	470,238	45.04
35-40-----------	.02015	93,123	461,211	38.14	.01705	93,457	463,543	40.54
40-45-----------	.02892	91,247	449,981	33.87	.02338	91,863	454,225	36.20
45-50-----------	.04112	88,608	434,361	29.80	.03204	89,715	441,730	32.01
50-55-----------	.05652	84,964	413,320	25.97	.04358	86,841	425,143	27.98
55-60-----------	.07707	80,162	385,981	22.37	.05993	83,057	403,336	24.13
60-65-----------	.10705	73,984	350,894	19.02	.08709	78,079	374,060	20.51
65-70-----------	.14666	66,064	306,773	15.99	.12279	71,279	335,125	17.22
70-75-----------	.20459	56,375	253,510	13.30	.17694	62,527	285,426	14.27
75-80-----------	.25575	44,841	195,328	11.06	.22771	51,463	227,808	11.79
80-85-----------	.31792	33,373	139,817	9.01	.29054	39,745	169,288	9.53
85 and over-----	1.00000	22,763	160,871	7.07	1.00000	28,198	209,490	7.43
	MALIGNANT NEOPLASMS OF DIGESTIVE ORGANS				MALIGNANT NEOPLASMS OF RESPIRATORY SYSTEM			
0-1--------------	0.02765	100,000	97,738	69.66	0.02765	100,000	97,738	69.25
1-5-------------	.00476	97,235	387,818	70.64	.00476	97,235	387,818	70.21
5-10------------	.00233	96,772	483,231	66.97	.00234	96,772	483,231	66.54
10-15-----------	.00200	96,546	482,300	62.12	.00200	96,546	482,300	61.69
15-20-----------	.00451	96,353	480,788	57.24	.00452	96,353	480,786	56.81
20-25-----------	.00695	95,918	478,008	52.49	.00698	95,917	477,998	52.05
25-30-----------	.00911	95,251	474,193	47.83	.00919	95,248	474,159	47.40
30-35-----------	.01303	94,384	469,047	43.25	.01314	94,373	468,966	42.81
35-40-----------	.01965	93,155	461,477	38.79	.01988	93,133	461,317	38.35
40-45-----------	.02802	91,324	450,556	34.51	.02832	91,281	450,279	34.07
45-50-----------	.03945	88,765	435,487	30.43	.04013	88,696	435,001	29.99
50-55-----------	.05367	85,264	415,361	26.57	.05513	85,136	414,441	26.13
55-60-----------	.07260	80,688	389,379	22.93	.07533	80,443	387,669	22.51
60-65-----------	.10117	74,830	355,962	19.52	.10538	74,383	353,084	19.13
65-70-----------	.13875	67,259	313,616	16.43	.14476	66,544	309,309	16.08
70-75-----------	.19448	57,927	261,929	13.66	.20231	56,911	256,239	13.36
75-80-----------	.24452	46,661	204,574	11.34	.25377	45,397	197,977	11.11
80-85-----------	.30730	35,251	148,639	9.21	.31617	33,877	142,080	9.04
85 and over-----	1.00000	24,418	176,109	7.21	1.00000	23,166	164,127	7.08

Table 5. ABRIDGED LIFE TABLES FOR ALL CAUSES OF DEATH COMBINED AND ELIMINATING SPECIFIED CAUSES OF DEATH, FOR FEMALES OTHER THAN WHITE: UNITED STATES, 1969-71—Con.

Period of life between two exact ages stated in years	Proportion of persons alive at beginning of age interval dying during interval	Of 100,000 born alive		Average number of years of life remaining at beginning of age interval	Proportion of persons alive at beginning of age interval dying during interval	Of 100,000 born alive		Average number of years of life remaining at beginning of age interval
		Number living at beginning of age interval	Stationary population in the age interval			Number living at beginning of age interval	Stationary population in the age interval	
x to $x+n$	$_nq_x$	ℓ_x	$_nL_x$	$\overset{\circ}{e}_x$	$_nq_x$	ℓ_x	$_nL_x$	$\overset{\circ}{e}_x$
	DIABETES				DISEASES OF THE HEART			
0-1----------------	0.02765	100,000	97,738	69.60	0.02738	100,000	97,760	75.33
1-5----------------	.00476	97,235	387,818	70.58	.00465	97,262	387,953	76.44
5-10---------------	.00233	96,772	483,234	66.91	.00225	96,810	483,443	72.79
10-15--------------	.00198	96,547	482,307	62.06	.00189	96,592	482,552	67.95
15-20--------------	.00448	96,355	480,805	57.18	.00427	96,409	481,120	63.07
20-25--------------	.00690	95,923	478,045	52.42	.00661	95,997	478,479	58.33
25-30--------------	.00908	95,261	474,248	47.77	.00843	95,362	474,900	53.70
30-35--------------	.01301	94,396	469,109	43.18	.01173	94,559	470,203	49.14
35-40--------------	.01973	93,168	461,525	38.72	.01710	93,450	463,499	44.69
40-45--------------	.02814	91,330	450,560	34.44	.02311	91,852	454,229	40.42
45-50--------------	.03972	88,760	435,402	30.36	.03144	89,729	441,926	36.31
50-55--------------	.05397	85,234	415,154	26.51	.04040	86,908	426,132	32.41
55-60--------------	.07278	80,634	389,083	22.87	.05265	83,397	406,445	28.66
60-65--------------	.10107	74,765	355,671	19.46	.06880	79,006	381,971	25.11
65-70--------------	.13910	67,208	313,319	16.36	.09165	73,570	351,463	21.77
70-75--------------	.19560	57,859	261,464	13.59	.12561	66,827	313,492	18.71
75-80--------------	.24691	46,542	203,773	11.28	.15455	58,433	269,424	16.04
80-85--------------	.30914	35,050	147,628	9.16	.19116	49,402	222,934	13.51
85 and over-----	1.00000	24,215	173,444	7.16	1.00000	39,958	444,644	11.13
	ISCHEMIC HEART DISEASE				ACUTE MYOCARDIAL INFARCTION			
0-1----------------	0.02764	100,000	97,739	73.94	0.02765	100,000	97,738	70.67
1-5----------------	.00476	97,236	387,822	75.04	.00476	97,235	387,818	71.68
5-10---------------	.00233	96,773	483,239	71.39	.00233	96,772	483,231	68.01
10-15--------------	.00199	96,548	482,310	66.55	.00200	96,546	482,300	63.17
15-20--------------	.00449	96,355	480,803	61.68	.00451	96,353	480,790	58.29
20-25--------------	.00690	95,922	478,040	56.94	.00693	95,919	478,018	53.54
25-30--------------	.00896	95,260	474,269	52.32	.00907	95,254	474,215	48.89
30-35--------------	.01250	94,406	469,272	47.77	.01282	94,390	469,121	44.32
35-40--------------	.01830	93,226	462,125	43.34	.01921	93,180	461,698	39.86
40-45--------------	.02495	91,520	452,190	39.10	.02697	91,390	451,108	35.59
45-50--------------	.03394	89,237	438,971	35.03	.03761	88,925	436,658	31.50
50-55--------------	.04387	86,208	421,983	31.17	.05049	85,580	417,552	27.63
55-60--------------	.05730	82,426	400,793	27.48	.06785	81,259	393,062	23.96
60-65--------------	.07493	77,703	374,529	23.99	.09264	75,746	361,873	20.52
65-70--------------	.09967	71,881	341,992	20.73	.12662	68,729	322,497	17.34
70-75--------------	.13629	64,716	301,889	17.74	.17851	60,027	273,784	14.49
75-80--------------	.16731	55,896	255,931	15.14	.22424	49,312	218,715	12.08
80-85--------------	.20730	46,544	208,124	12.68	.28079	38,254	163,888	9.86
85 and over-----	1.00000	36,896	381,965	10.35	1.00000	27,513	213,186	7.75

Table 5. ABRIDGED LIFE TABLES FOR ALL CAUSES OF DEATH COMBINED AND ELIMINATING SPECIFIED CAUSES OF DEATH, FOR FEMALES OTHER THAN WHITE: UNITED STATES, 1969-71—Con.

Period of life between two exact ages stated in years	Proportion of persons alive at beginning of age interval dying during interval	Of 100,000 born alive		Average number of years of life remaining at beginning of age interval	Proportion of persons alive at beginning of age interval dying during interval	Of 100,000 born alive		Average number of years of life remaining at beginning of age interval
		Number living at beginning of age interval	Stationary population in the age interval			Number living at beginning of age interval	Stationary population in the age interval	
x to $x+n$	$_nq_x$	ℓ_x	$_nL_x$	$\overset{\circ}{e}_x$	$_nq_x$	ℓ_x	$_nL_x$	$\overset{\circ}{e}_x$
	CEREBROVASCULAR DISEASES				ARTERIOSCLEROSIS			
0-1	0.02758	100,000	97,744	71.21	0.02765	100,000	97,738	69.21
1-5	.00472	97,242	387,855	72.22	.00476	97,235	387,818	70.18
5-10	.00230	96,783	483,294	68.56	.00234	96,772	483,231	66.50
10-15	.00196	96,560	482,379	63.71	.00200	96,546	482,300	61.65
15-20	.00443	96,371	480,896	58.83	.00453	96,353	480,786	56.77
20-25	.00680	95,944	478,171	54.08	.00698	95,917	477,996	52.02
25-30	.00878	95,291	474,464	49.43	.00920	95,247	474,149	47.37
30-35	.01229	94,454	469,556	44.85	.01321	94,370	468,935	42.78
35-40	.01854	93,293	462,404	40.37	.02013	93,123	461,213	38.32
40-45	.02627	91,563	452,113	36.08	.02889	91,248	449,993	34.05
45-50	.03666	89,157	437,999	31.99	.04107	88,612	434,393	29.99
50-55	.05016	85,888	419,123	28.10	.05638	84,973	413,391	26.16
55-60	.06792	81,580	394,600	24.45	.07675	80,182	386,139	22.57
60-65	.09234	76,039	363,326	21.04	.10637	74,028	351,225	19.23
65-70	.12411	69,017	324,267	17.92	.14528	66,154	307,413	16.20
70-75	.17091	60,451	276,846	15.10	.20138	56,543	254,714	13.52
75-80	.21142	50,119	223,914	12.68	.25100	45,157	197,243	11.29
80-85	.26398	39,523	171,018	10.42	.31037	33,822	142,350	9.24
85 and over	1.00000	29,090	240,788	8.28	1.00000	23,325	170,254	7.30
	DISEASES OF RESPIRATORY SYSTEM				INFLUENZA AND PNEUMONIA			
0-1	0.02355	100,000	98,073	70.01	0.02430	100,000	98,012	69.75
1-5	.00402	97,645	389,651	70.69	.00423	97,570	389,298	70.48
5-10	.00215	97,252	485,678	66.97	.00220	97,157	485,189	66.77
10-15	.00184	97,043	484,818	62.11	.00189	96,943	484,307	61.92
15-20	.00428	96,865	483,393	57.22	.00438	96,760	482,850	57.03
20-25	.00660	96,450	480,742	52.46	.00676	96,337	480,141	52.27
25-30	.00868	95,814	477,091	47.79	.00889	95,686	476,406	47.60
30-35	.01243	94,982	472,149	43.18	.01276	94,835	471,346	43.01
35-40	.01905	93,801	464,810	38.69	.01948	93,625	463,843	38.53
40-45	.02741	92,014	454,093	34.39	.02796	91,801	452,922	34.24
45-50	.03918	89,492	439,110	30.29	.03991	89,234	437,686	30.15
50-55	.05433	85,986	418,744	26.42	.05521	85,672	417,032	26.30
55-60	.07414	81,315	392,104	22.78	.07524	80,942	390,092	22.68
60-65	.10367	75,286	357,680	19.40	.10475	74,852	355,424	19.31
65-70	.14214	67,481	314,094	16.34	.14345	67,011	311,693	16.27
70-75	.19831	57,889	261,213	13.63	.19972	57,398	258,797	13.56
75-80	.24783	46,409	203,082	11.37	.24941	45,934	200,821	11.31
80-85	.30743	34,907	147,176	9.30	.30920	34,477	145,210	9.25
85 and over	1.00000	24,175	177,365	7.34	1.00000	23,817	173,694	7.29

Period of life between two exact ages stated in years	Proportion of persons alive at beginning of age interval dying during interval	Of 100,000 born alive		Average number of years of life remaining at beginning of age interval	Proportion of persons alive at beginning of age interval dying during interval	Of 100,000 born alive		Average number of years of life remaining at beginning of age interval
		Number living at beginning of age interval	Stationary population in the age interval			Number living at beginning of age interval	Stationary population in the age interval	
x to $x+n$	$_nq_x$	ℓ_x	$_nL_x$	$\overset{\circ}{e}_x$	$_nq_x$	ℓ_x	$_nL_x$	$\overset{\circ}{e}_x$
BRONCHITIS, EMPHYSEMA, AND ASTHMA					CIRRHOSIS OF LIVER			
0-1	0.02758	100,000	97,744	69.15	0.02764	100,000	97,739	69.40
1-5	.00470	97,242	387,862	70.11	.00475	97,236	387,825	70.37
5-10	.00231	96,785	483,304	66.43	.00233	96,774	483,241	66.70
10-15	.00197	96,562	482,384	61.58	.00199	96,548	482,312	61.85
15-20	.00447	96,371	480,887	56.70	.00449	96,356	480,808	56.97
20-25	.00690	95,940	478,130	51.94	.00690	95,923	478,045	52.21
25-30	.00909	95,278	474,330	47.28	.00881	95,261	474,309	47.56
30-35	.01307	94,412	469,175	42.69	.01222	94,422	469,412	42.96
35-40	.01993	93,178	461,531	38.22	.01848	93,268	462,293	38.45
40-45	.02865	91,321	450,406	33.95	.02678	91,544	451,909	34.13
45-50	.04073	88,705	434,920	29.87	.03885	89,092	437,217	30.00
50-55	.05606	85,092	414,037	26.03	.05445	85,631	416,988	26.10
55-60	.07651	80,322	386,858	22.42	.07533	80,968	390,201	22.46
60-65	.10649	74,176	351,904	19.06	.10572	74,869	355,331	19.07
65-70	.14606	66,277	307,860	16.02	.14564	66,954	311,072	16.02
70-75	.20396	56,597	254,595	13.32	.20400	57,203	257,318	13.31
75-80	.25498	45,053	196,338	11.08	.25514	45,534	198,418	11.07
80-85	.31708	33,565	140,693	9.03	.31756	33,917	142,127	9.02
85 and over	1.00000	22,922	162,285	7.08	1.00000	23,146	163,675	7.07
MOTOR VEHICLE ACCIDENTS					ALL OTHER ACCIDENTS			
0-1	0.02756	100,000	97,745	69.42	0.02670	100,000	97,816	69.59
1-5	.00424	97,244	387,951	70.39	.00363	97,330	388,460	70.49
5-10	.00177	96,832	483,681	66.68	.00180	96,977	484,398	66.74
10-15	.00170	96,660	482,935	61.79	.00160	96,802	483,665	61.86
15-20	.00378	96,496	481,663	56.89	.00401	96,647	482,366	56.95
20-25	.00602	96,132	479,287	52.10	.00638	96,260	479,844	52.17
25-30	.00843	95,553	475,850	47.40	.00857	95,646	476,282	47.49
30-35	.01244	94,748	470,984	42.78	.01256	94,827	471,351	42.88
35-40	.01938	93,569	463,589	38.28	.01933	93,636	463,931	38.39
40-45	.02811	91,756	452,668	33.99	.02813	91,826	453,009	34.09
45-50	.04037	89,177	437,311	29.90	.04020	89,243	437,669	30.00
50-55	.05564	85,577	416,483	26.04	.05549	85,655	416,892	26.15
55-60	.07632	80,816	389,275	22.42	.07606	80,902	389,741	22.54
60-65	.10629	74,648	354,180	19.06	.10564	74,749	354,777	19.18
65-70	.14593	66,714	309,911	16.02	.14472	66,853	310,752	16.13
70-75	.20378	56,979	256,341	13.32	.20203	57,178	257,481	13.43
75-80	.25510	45,368	197,699	11.08	.25222	45,626	199,152	11.19
80-85	.31745	33,795	141,626	9.02	.31317	34,118	143,351	9.12
85 and over	1.00000	23,067	163,169	7.07	1.00000	23,433	167,909	7.17

Table 6. NUMBER OF LIFE-TABLE DEATHS FROM SPECIFIED CAUSES FOR THE TOTAL POPULATION: UNITED STATES, 1969-71

Period of life between two exact ages stated in years	Of 10,000,000 born alive number dying during age interval from specified cause							
	Number living at beginning of age interval	Malignant neoplasms	Malignant neoplasms of digestive organs	Malignant neoplasms of respiratory system	Diabetes	Diseases of the heart	Ischemic heart disease	Acute myocardial infarction
0-1----------	10,000,000	441	37	12	41	1,276	62	43
1-5-----------	9,799,800	2,877	76	21	57	647	26	12
5-10----------	9,766,800	3,306	26	16	82	413	42	25
10-15---------	9,746,000	2,539	38	31	143	494	46	24
15-20---------	9,726,100	3,464	118	56	199	1,152	163	96
20-25---------	9,671,600	4,430	310	116	457	1,829	470	320
25-30---------	9,600,000	6,141	625	232	880	3,333	1,420	946
30-35---------	9,530,700	10,272	1,443	846	1,425	7,720	4,792	3,356
35-40---------	9,448,200	18,926	2,963	2,869	2,052	19,380	14,491	10,261
40-45---------	9,332,200	35,679	6,244	7,532	2,825	41,863	34,243	24,694
45-50---------	9,158,700	62,341	12,162	14,972	4,297	78,811	67,325	48,410
50-55---------	8,897,200	99,389	22,275	26,081	7,151	134,456	117,958	83,408
55-60---------	8,511,000	146,633	36,571	40,309	11,414	212,030	188,708	130,048
60-65---------	7,952,900	188,928	51,023	51,346	17,569	309,333	279,002	184,550
65-70---------	7,193,300	227,507	67,036	57,478	25,245	423,259	386,275	241,685
70-75---------	6,198,400	240,756	77,295	51,797	32,014	544,632	501,866	286,543
75-80---------	4,970,500	234,963	81,383	39,646	36,036	655,757	606,566	307,529
80-85---------	3,528,500	180,178	66,683	22,138	30,958	672,893	621,607	266,407
85 and over---	2,090,800	161,247	61,616	13,721	27,931	1,011,305	927,772	300,846

Table 6. NUMBER OF LIFE-TABLE DEATHS FROM SPECIFIED CAUSES FOR THE TOTAL POPULATION: UNITED STATES, 1969-71—Con.

Period of life between two exact ages stated in years	Of 10,000,000 born alive number dying during age interval from specified cause—Con.							
	Cerebro-vascular diseases	Arterio-sclerosis	Diseases of respiratory system	Influenza and pneumonia	Bronchitis, emphysema, and asthma	Cirrhosis of liver	Motor vehicle accidents	All other accidents
0-1------------	444	2	21,232	17,328	393	88	985	5,428
1-5------------	386	1	4,449	3,009	312	77	4,520	7,815
5-10----------	283	2	1,293	853	121	58	5,272	4,519
10-15---------	357	2	1,060	711	154	60	4,707	5,132
15-20---------	628	1	1,625	1,038	205	153	21,790	9,873
20-25---------	988	5	2,100	1,313	262	312	25,237	10,705
25-30---------	1,606	12	2,422	1,571	323	1,117	16,499	9,682
30-35---------	2,999	18	3,241	2,029	452	3,175	13,154	9,809
35-40---------	5,393	48	4,894	3,062	818	6,601	11,869	10,392
40-45---------	8,844	159	7,402	4,422	1,525	11,103	11,239	11,145
45-50---------	14,534	318	11,411	6,114	2,959	15,322	10,933	11,670
50-55---------	22,613	742	17,751	8,404	5,751	18,428	11,163	12,801
55-60---------	35,081	1,680	28,467	11,713	10,892	19,976	11,136	13,629
60-65---------	56,826	3,653	42,724	16,055	17,742	18,829	10,603	14,737
65-70---------	93,296	7,569	58,661	22,232	24,681	15,366	10,416	15,175
70-75---------	145,915	15,615	74,641	32,700	28,729	10,163	10,165	17,085
75-80---------	208,588	28,250	86,997	45,948	27,241	6,812	9,226	21,519
80-85---------	243,815	44,631	84,050	54,529	18,755	3,927	6,237	25,679
85 and over---	381,833	118,437	136,595	109,493	15,131	2,380	3,944	47,469

Table 7. NUMBER OF LIFE-TABLE DEATHS FROM SPECIFIED CAUSES FOR WHITE MALES: UNITED STATES, 1969-71

Period of life between two exact ages stated in years	Of 10,000,000 born alive number dying during age interval from specified cause							
	Number living at beginning of age interval	Malignant neoplasms	Malignant neoplasms of digestive organs	Malignant neoplasms of respiratory system	Diabetes	Diseases of the heart	Ischemic heart disease	Acute myocardial infarction
0-1-----------	10,000,000	458	48	6	39	1,106	71	54
1-5-----------	9,799,400	3,305	83	17	64	551	24	6
5-10----------	9,767,100	3,959	25	19	91	351	38	28
10-15---------	9,744,100	2,903	32	38	99	420	47	20
15-20---------	9,720,800	4,318	143	76	151	1,207	178	113
20-25---------	9,648,000	5,739	340	156	414	1,800	522	372
25-30---------	9,552,400	6,784	666	296	790	3,298	1,687	1,191
30-35---------	9,471,600	9,383	1,482	1,061	1,479	8,788	6,395	4,891
35-40---------	9,384,300	15,813	2,984	3,598	1,953	25,919	21,699	16,662
40-45---------	9,263,100	29,699	6,184	10,173	2,734	60,436	53,219	41,084
45-50---------	9,072,500	54,307	12,650	20,740	3,892	119,012	107,610	82,228
50-55---------	8,769,000	95,887	24,010	37,955	6,206	203,176	185,769	139,568
55-60---------	8,300,100	156,766	40,710	63,363	9,665	313,128	288,243	210,076
60-65---------	7,596,900	217,160	58,067	85,893	14,610	433,808	401,551	280,874
65-70---------	6,634,300	267,438	74,633	99,416	20,137	551,472	513,470	342,191
70-75---------	5,413,800	273,752	80,989	88,096	23,924	627,244	586,535	358,884
75-80---------	4,032,400	248,901	78,786	63,192	25,188	655,546	612,982	335,359
80-85---------	2,588,500	171,822	56,916	31,655	19,903	570,901	532,009	247,972
85 and over---	1,352,700	125,950	42,899	15,655	15,917	645,122	595,429	218,197

Table 7. NUMBER OF LIFE-TABLE DEATHS FROM SPECIFIED CAUSES FOR WHITE MALES: UNITED STATES, 1969-71—Con.

Period of life between two exact ages stated in years	Of 10,000,000 born alive number dying during age interval from specified cause—Con.							
	Cerebro-vascular diseases	Arterio-sclerosis	Diseases of respiratory system	Influenza and pneumonia	Bronchitis, emphysema, and asthma	Cirrhosis of liver	Motor vehicle accidents	All other accidents
0-1------------	428	0	18,542	15,115	376	93	977	5,056
1-5------------	426	0	3,984	2,539	278	66	4,655	8,374
5-10-----------	279	6	1,247	787	102	42	6,007	5,447
10-15----------	363	0	959	646	127	36	6,101	7,047
15-20----------	626	2	1,571	994	162	113	33,569	15,227
20-25----------	890	7	2,062	1,352	163	191	41,553	16,999
25-30----------	1,272	8	1,959	1,304	175	738	25,469	14,584
30-35----------	2,033	29	2,400	1,520	309	2,626	19,067	14,407
35-40----------	3,731	45	3,854	2,380	618	5,989	16,753	15,020
40-45----------	6,594	179	6,723	3,832	1,554	11,812	15,376	15,870
45-50----------	11,665	382	11,855	6,024	3,442	18,026	14,948	16,466
50-55----------	19,861	858	21,054	8,971	7,758	23,105	14,771	17,571
55-60----------	33,565	2,030	37,927	13,505	16,504	26,761	14,670	19,145
60-65----------	57,220	4,389	62,537	19,419	29,607	26,419	13,583	20,056
65-70----------	92,508	8,224	88,564	26,806	43,390	21,728	12,950	19,266
70-75----------	137,259	15,695	108,929	38,567	50,179	13,562	12,025	19,027
75-80----------	179,698	25,594	114,496	49,748	45,024	8,123	10,801	20,157
80-85----------	183,735	35,882	93,051	51,118	28,288	4,246	7,253	19,958
85 and over---	218,372	69,112	104,731	75,891	18,002	2,267	4,502	29,007

Table 8. NUMBER OF LIFE-TABLE DEATHS FROM SPECIFIED CAUSES FOR WHITE FEMALES: UNITED STATES, 1969-71

Period of life between two exact ages stated in years	Of 10,000,000 born alive number dying during age interval from specified cause							
	Number living at beginning of age interval	Malignant neoplasms	Malignant neoplasms of digestive organs	Malignant neoplasms of respiratory system	Diabetes	Diseases of the heart	Ischemic heart disease	Acute myocardial infarction
0-1-----------	10,000,000	476	32	16	46	867	43	27
1-5-----------	9,846,800	2,671	73	23	51	509	11	9
5-10----------	9,820,300	2,956	30	16	85	365	38	22
10-15---------	9,804,200	2,271	42	19	191	387	42	23
15-20---------	9,790,200	2,674	73	36	204	674	87	44
20-25---------	9,761,800	3,310	228	82	422	1,089	217	141
25-30---------	9,729,900	5,445	454	144	791	1,742	552	364
30-35---------	9,694,500	10,566	1,157	550	1,147	3,445	1,537	1,026
35-40---------	9,647,400	20,316	2,419	1,712	1,421	7,283	4,189	2,932
40-45---------	9,576,200	38,383	5,280	3,918	1,784	15,170	10,289	7,301
45-50---------	9,464,900	65,607	9,856	7,832	3,108	29,784	21,697	15,307
50-55---------	9,292,400	97,501	18,254	12,528	5,445	55,319	43,761	29,546
55-60---------	9,038,300	132,678	29,789	16,337	9,588	100,977	83,848	56,045
60-65---------	8,672,600	160,806	42,068	17,575	16,464	176,512	152,806	98,604
65-70---------	8,157,900	193,735	59,846	18,065	26,893	296,890	266,166	161,656
70-75---------	7,410,100	215,764	75,529	16,861	38,830	476,836	436,445	239,790
75-80---------	6,329,000	233,220	89,200	15,544	49,180	698,894	643,561	309,070
80-85---------	4,818,200	199,891	82,869	11,484	45,727	846,357	779,818	314,298
85 and over---	3,049,000	204,096	85,616	10,563	42,997	1,497,707	1,374,320	412,433

Table 8. NUMBER OF LIFE-TABLE DEATHS FROM SPECIFIED CAUSES FOR WHITE FEMALES: UNITED STATES, 1969-71—Con.

Period of life between two exact ages stated in years	Of 10,000,000 born alive number dying during age interval from specified cause—Con.							
	Cerebro-vascular diseases	Arterio-sclerosis	Diseases of respiratory system	Influenza and pneumonia	Bronchitis, emphysema, and asthma	Cirrhosis of liver	Motor vehicle accidents	All other accidents
0-1-----------	318	5	13,755	11,149	263	80	995	3,757
1-5-----------	288	2	3,324	2,258	209	75	3,845	5,282
5-10----------	280	0	1,154	805	87	81	3,700	2,511
10-15---------	319	4	961	670	121	77	3,312	2,104
15-20---------	496	0	1,219	848	127	155	12,085	2,584
20-25---------	857	2	1,436	888	212	212	9,971	2,586
25-30---------	1,263	14	1,796	1,155	277	475	6,655	2,688
30-35---------	2,371	10	2,314	1,390	367	1,217	5,890	3,091
35-40---------	4,302	32	3,256	1,973	617	3,400	5,881	3,525
40-45---------	6,645	85	4,981	2,820	1,137	6,606	6,004	4,306
45-50---------	11,094	187	7,574	3,724	2,147	9,956	6,024	5,115
50-55---------	16,894	432	11,426	5,509	3,614	12,562	6,704	6,207
55-60---------	25,536	1,027	16,366	7,392	5,637	13,212	6,938	6,957
60-65---------	42,662	2,393	22,058	10,163	7,546	11,982	7,180	8,162
65-70---------	77,784	6,171	30,340	15,393	9,233	10,132	7,941	10,063
70-75---------	145,614	14,978	42,434	25,311	10,397	7,752	8,760	14,539
75-80---------	245,661	32,743	61,615	42,902	10,531	6,047	8,079	23,857
80-85---------	330,373	58,947	78,656	61,588	9,020	3,955	5,401	34,359
85 and over---	596,230	187,486	178,459	154,083	11,500	2,506	3,092	72,620

Table 9. NUMBER OF LIFE-TABLE DEATHS FROM SPECIFIED CAUSES FOR MALES OTHER THAN WHITE: UNITED STATES, 1969-71

Period of life between two exact ages stated in years	Of 10,000,000 born alive number dying during age interval from specified cause							
	Number living at beginning of age interval	Malignant neoplasms	Malignant neoplasms of digestive organs	Malignant neoplasms of respiratory system	Diabetes	Diseases of the heart	Ischemic heart disease	Acute myocardial infarction
0-1-----------	10,000,000	347	32	32	42	2,599	84	74
1-5-----------	9,659,200	2,185	80	11	22	1,312	92	35
5-10----------	9,603,800	2,682	32	21	21	644	74	21
10-15---------	9,571,600	2,407	52	63	125	1,001	73	52
15-20---------	9,538,500	3,795	218	73	255	2,377	352	243
20-25---------	9,429,300	4,454	704	115	672	5,587	1,655	1,049
25-30---------	9,226,700	5,870	1,226	462	1,809	10,859	4,866	3,037
30-35---------	9,010,600	10,138	2,800	1,626	2,439	23,154	14,208	8,449
35-40---------	8,759,700	20,168	4,880	6,459	5,205	49,348	33,772	18,829
40-45---------	8,437,800	43,957	11,888	17,262	6,691	92,034	70,544	40,431
45-50---------	8,016,300	81,750	23,946	33,001	8,483	146,532	118,240	64,597
50-55---------	7,474,800	132,323	38,434	53,567	13,452	213,908	178,281	96,770
55-60---------	6,780,800	180,274	55,656	67,979	16,105	283,104	238,564	123,195
60-65---------	5,939,600	211,564	67,525	70,750	21,669	350,977	301,468	149,503
65-70---------	4,960,700	220,621	69,247	66,618	22,662	398,338	344,572	162,753
70-75---------	3,902,500	217,020	70,643	53,062	23,586	438,702	381,773	167,017
75-80---------	2,778,900	172,311	54,601	34,382	19,907	390,806	344,592	140,839
80-85---------	1,799,900	111,388	35,658	17,517	11,818	291,515	257,350	97,824
85 and over---	1,081,100	111,919	35,948	13,772	12,498	469,518	412,952	140,987

Table 9. NUMBER OF LIFE-TABLE DEATHS FROM SPECIFIED CAUSES FOR MALES OTHER THAN WHITE: UNITED STATES, 1969-71—Con.

Period of life between two exact ages stated in years	Of 10,000,000 born alive number dying during age interval from specified cause—Con.							
	Cerebro-vascular diseases	Arterio-sclerosis	Diseases of respiratory system	Influenza and pneumonia	Bronchitis, emphysema, and asthma	Cirrhosis of liver	Motor vehicle accidents	All other accidents
0-1------------	810	0	49,107	40,437	810	84	1,063	.10,881
1-5------------	627	0	9,690	7,062	736	78	6,648	14,160
5-10----------	275	0	1,817	1,088	275	42	9,456	9,486
10-15----------	511	10	1,668	938	396	52	6,058	11,949
15-20---------	1,164	0	3,675	2,050	643	194	21,887	25,452
20-25---------	1,851	0	5,520	3,260	704	1,408	40,935	31,918
25-30---------	3,962	0	7,661	5,067	844	5,749	32,988	29,132
30-35---------	7,771	0	11,022	7,543	1,061	13,820	29,057	28,743
35-40---------	14,319	70	18,152	12,271	2,347	23,933	25,296	29,787
40-45---------	25,702	468	23,981	16,307	3,144	30,667	23,968	31,740
45-50---------	38,428	640	32,413	20,989	5,058	31,832	22,921	29,844
50-55---------	58,034	1,871	40,712	24,052	8,631	28,656	21,557	31,252
55-60---------	80,786	2,974	50,874	27,231	13,269	24,062	20,225	26,391
60-65---------	104,492	5,700	58,124	31,597	14,532	18,998	17,140	25,636
65-70---------	136,394	9,859	61,548	34,033	15,829	12,966	13,499	21,164
70-75---------	154,990	15,009	69,239	40,570	15,939	6,578	9,833	20,311
75-80---------	144,199	17,343	64,912	40,319	13,945	3,370	7,649	15,749
80-85---------	113,440	17,617	47,554	32,208	8,913	1,520	4,391	11,731
85 and over---	174,140	42,878	76,476	57,167	9,640	1,515	3,029	20,757

Table 10. NUMBER OF LIFE-TABLE DEATHS FROM SPECIFIED CAUSES FOR FEMALES OTHER THAN WHITE: UNITED STATES, 1969-71

Period of life between two exact ages stated in years	Of 10,000,000 born alive number dying during age interval from specified cause							
	Number living at beginning of age interval	Malignant neoplasms	Malignant neoplasms of digestive organs	Malignant neoplasms of respiratory system	Diabetes	Diseases of the heart	Ischemic heart disease	Acute myocardial infarction
0-1-----------	10,000,000	293	11	0	33	2,710	76	33
1-5-----------	9,723,500	2,269	34	24	82	1,157	23	23
5-10----------	9,677,200	2,187	11	0	75	808	54	22
10-15---------	9,654,600	1,994	31	21	147	1,008	42	21
15-20---------	9,635,300	2,611	144	36	409	2,455	337	156
20-25---------	9,591,700	3,639	321	88	789	3,610	775	526
25-30---------	9,524,700	6,881	975	181	1,264	7,479	2,348	1,319
30-35---------	9,437,000	14,108	1,788	664	1,929	14,110	6,754	3,779
35-40---------	9,312,300	29,036	4,633	2,452	3,934	28,568	17,383	8,775
40-45---------	9,124,700	51,131	8,298	5,584	7,204	53,637	36,711	18,044
45-50---------	8,860,800	81,861	15,179	8,972	12,670	87,183	64,763	31,715
50-55---------	8,496,400	112,454	24,882	12,166	22,275	139,858	109,931	52,587
55-60---------	8,016,200	141,706	37,181	14,463	35,691	201,154	163,245	76,605
60-65---------	7,398,400	154,654	45,908	13,050	46,655	293,378	247,230	111,995
65-70---------	6,606,400	168,546	56,358	13,569	53,888	381,635	327,460	141,828
70-75---------	5,637,500	172,196	63,680	14,422	56,674	477,021	415,131	162,594
75-80---------	4,484,100	143,593	58,119	10,323	45,826	494,964	435,944	160,961
80-85---------	3,337,300	109,163	42,840	7,113	35,491	472,681	416,799	146,999
85 and over---	2,276,300	149,399	61,809	7,526	40,974	1,056,562	932,671	275,469

Table 10. NUMBER OF LIFE-TABLE DEATHS FROM SPECIFIED CAUSES FOR FEMALES OTHER THAN WHITE: UNITED STATES, 1969-71--Con.

Period of life between two exact ages stated in years	Of 10,000,000 born alive number dying during age interval from specified cause—Con.							
	Cerebro-vascular diseases	Arterio-sclerosis	Diseases of respiratory system	Influenza and pneumonia	Bronchitis, emphysema, and asthma	Cirrhosis of liver	Motor vehicle accidents	All other accidents
0-1------------	748	0	41,488	33,931	672	108	900	9,604
1-5------------	424	0	7,128	5,074	577	150	5,049	11,080
5-10----------	334	0	1,800	1,272	259	43	5,464	5,157
10-15---------	378	0	1,576	1,082	242	115	2,898	3,847
15-20----------	903	0	2,360	1,444	494	337	7,220	5,011
20-25----------	1,740	15	3,744	2,178	833	774	9,268	5,810
25-30----------	4,047	36	5,043	3,035	1,157	3,792	7,480	6,131
30-35---------	8,785	20	7,441	4,342	1,347	9,463	7,337	6,178
35-40---------	15,099	144	10,283	6,221	2,040	15,626	7,189	7,650
40-45----------	24,498	264	13,949	8,890	2,558	19,778	7,510	7,355
45-50----------	40,293	542	17,575	10,962	3,597	20,547	6,845	8,327
50-55----------	55,436	1,165	19,151	11,449	4,015	18,042	7,696	8,988
55-60----------	75,968	2,695	24,400	15,271	4,625	14,500	6,250	8,444
60-65---------	114,285	5,353	26,425	17,984	4,395	10,419	5,949	11,037
65-70---------	159,318	9,859	32,296	22,952	4,313	7,310	5,240	13,906
70-75----------	208,978	20,340	39,650	30,758	4,018	3,779	5,165	16,223
75-80----------	224,612	24,677	41,083	32,906	3,979	3,189	3,398	18,337
80-85---------	211,082	30,514	42,322	35,249	3,405	1,451	1,903	19,246
85 and over---	452,204	103,864	118,785	100,549	5,759	1,836	2,824	43,449

Table 11. PROBABILITY OF EVENTUALLY DYING FROM SPECIFIED CAUSES FOR THE TOTAL POPULATION: UNITED STATES, 1969-71

Exact age in years	Probability for persons at the indicated exact age of eventually dying from the specified cause							
	Malignant neoplasms	Malignant neoplasms of digestive organs	Malignant neoplasms of respiratory system	Diabetes	Diseases of the heart	Ischemic heart disease	Acute myocardial infarction	Cerebro-vascular diseases
0--------------	0.16300	0.04879	0.03292	0.02008	0.41206	0.37528	0.18892	0.12244
1--------------	.16629	.04979	.03359	.02048	.42035	.38294	.19278	.12490
5--------------	.16655	.04995	.03370	.02055	.42170	.38423	.19343	.12528
10-------------	.16657	.05005	.03377	.02058	.42256	.38505	.19384	.12552
15-------------	.16665	.05015	.03384	.02061	.42337	.38583	.19423	.12574
20-------------	.16723	.05042	.03403	.02071	.42564	.38799	.19531	.12638
25-------------	.16802	.05076	.03427	.02081	.42862	.39084	.19674	.12722
30-------------	.16859	.05107	.03449	.02087	.43139	.39353	.19807	.12798
35-------------	.16898	.05136	.03470	.02090	.43434	.39646	.19944	.12878
40-------------	.16905	.05168	.03483	.02094	.43766	.39983	.20082	.12980
45-------------	.16836	.05198	.03467	.02103	.44138	.40367	.20193	.13130
50-------------	.16630	.05214	.03400	.02117	.44550	.40797	.20243	.13352
55-------------	.16217	.05189	.03248	.02129	.44991	.41262	.20181	.13692
60-------------	.15511	.05093	.02969	.02134	.45483	.41785	.19962	.14212
65-------------	.14523	.04921	.02569	.02116	.45985	.42318	.19504	.14923
70-------------	.13183	.04630	.02054	.02048	.46538	.42879	.18736	.15813
75-------------	.11596	.04219	.01519	.01910	.47077	.43375	.17599	.16784
80-------------	.09676	.03636	.01016	.01669	.47731	.43910	.16076	.17731
85-------------	.07712	.02947	.00656	.01336	.48369	.44374	.14389	.18263

5-48

Table 11. PROBABILITY OF EVENTUALLY DYING FROM SPECIFIED CAUSES FOR THE TOTAL POPULATION: UNITED STATES, 1969-71—Con.

Exact age in years	Probability for persons at the indicated exact age of eventually dying from the specified cause—Con.						
	Arterio-sclerosis	Diseases of respiratory system	Influenza and pneumonia	Bronchitis, emphysema, and asthma	Cirrhosis of liver	Motor vehicle accidents	All other accidents
0--------------------	0.02211	0.05910	0.03425	0.01564	0.01339	0.01991	0.02643
1--------------------	.02257	.05814	.03318	.01592	.01366	.02022	.02641
5--------------------	.02264	.05788	.03299	.01595	.01370	.01982	.02570
10-------------------	.02269	.05787	.03297	.01597	.01372	.01932	.02529
15-------------------	.02274	.05788	.03297	.01598	.01374	.01888	.02482
20-------------------	.02286	.05804	.03304	.01605	.01380	.01673	.02394
25-------------------	.02303	.05826	.03315	.01615	.01387	.01423	.02300
30-------------------	.02320	.05843	.03323	.01623	.01386	.01260	.02215
35-------------------	.02340	.05859	.03330	.01632	.01364	.01132	.02131
40-------------------	.02369	.05880	.03339	.01644	.01311	.01019	.02046
45-------------------	.02412	.05910	.03354	.01658	.01214	.00915	.01963
50-------------------	.02479	.05956	.03384	.01674	.01078	.00819	.01889
55-------------------	.02583	.06017	.03439	.01682	.00910	.00725	.01825
60-------------------	.02743	.06082	.03533	.01663	.00723	.00636	.01781
65-------------------	.02982	.06130	.03683	.01592	.00537	.00556	.01765
70-------------------	.03338	.06167	.03915	.01450	.00376	.00477	.01803
75-------------------	.03849	.06189	.04224	.01230	.00264	.00390	.01905
80-------------------	.04621	.06253	.04648	.00960	.00179	.00289	.02073
85-------------------	.05665	.06533	.05237	.00724	.00114	.00189	.02270

TABLE. 12. PROBABILITY OF EVENTUALLY DYING FROM SPECIFIED CAUSES FOR WHITE MALES: UNITED STATES, 1969-71

Exact age in years	Probability for persons at the indicated exact age of eventually dying from the specified cause							
	Malignant neoplasms	Malignant neoplasms of digestive organs	Malignant neoplasms of respiratory system	Diabetes	Diseases of the heart	Ischemic heart disease	Acute myocardial infarction	Cerebro-vascular diseases
0--------------	0.16943	0.04816	0.05214	0.01473	0.42233	0.39075	0.22798	0.09505
1--------------	.17286	.04915	.05321	.01502	.43086	.39874	.23264	.09695
5--------------	.17309	.04930	.05338	.01507	.43223	.40006	.23341	.09723
10-------------	.17309	.04941	.05351	.01509	.43321	.40100	.23396	.09743
15-------------	.17321	.04953	.05363	.01512	.43421	.40195	.23451	.09763
20-------------	.17407	.04989	.05403	.01522	.43736	.40497	.23627	.09830
25-------------	.17521	.05035	.05455	.01533	.44155	.40897	.23860	.09919
30-------------	.17599	.05071	.05499	.01537	.44497	.41228	.24051	.09990
35-------------	.17662	.05102	.05538	.01536	.44817	.41543	.24222	.10062
40-------------	.17723	.05137	.05572	.01535	.45124	.41852	.24359	.10153
45-------------	.17768	.05177	.05577	.01537	.45405	.42145	.24418	.10294
50-------------	.17763	.05212	.05533	.01546	.45620	.42376	.24326	.10517
55-------------	.17612	.05217	.05389	.01558	.45749	.42532	.24018	.10872
60-------------	.17178	.05164	.05053	.01575	.45862	.42675	.23476	.11436
65-------------	.16398	.05038	.04492	.01584	.45977	.42814	.22649	.12233
70-------------	.15154	.04795	.03668	.01569	.46156	.42982	.21434	.13282
75-------------	.13557	.04429	.02740	.01513	.46413	.43161	.19877	.14428
80-------------	.11504	.03856	.01828	.01384	.46978	.43556	.18009	.15534
85-------------	.09311	.03171	.01157	.01177	.47691	.44018	.16130	.16143

TABLE 12. PROBABILITY OF EVENTUALLY DYING FROM SPECIFIED CAUSES ·FOR WHITE MALES: UNITED STATES, 1969-71—Con.

| Exact age in years | Probability for persons at the indicated exact age of eventually dying from the specified cause—Con. | | | | | | |
	Arterio-sclerosis	Diseases of respiratory system	Influenza and pneumonia	Bronchitis, emphysema, and asthma	Cirrhosis of liver	Motor vehicle accidents	All other accidents
0---------------	0.01624	0.06864	0.03205	0.02461	0.01659	0.02750	0.02987
1---------------	.01658	.06816	.03117	.02507	.01692	.02797	.02996
5---------------	.01663	.06798	.03101	.02513	.01697	.02758	.02921
10--------------	.01667	.06801	.03100	.02517	.01701	.02703	.02872
15--------------	.01671	.06807	.03101	.02522	.01705	.02647	.02806
20--------------	.01684	.06842	.03114	.02540	.01716	.02319	.02669
25--------------	.01700	.06889	.03131	.02563	.01732	.01907	.02518
30--------------	.01715	.06927	.03144	.02583	.01739	.01654	.02386
35--------------	.01730	.06966	.03157	.02604	.01727	.01467	.02254
40--------------	.01753	.07016	.03173	.02631	.01685	.01305	.02122
45--------------	.01787	.07089	.03197	.02670	.01590	.01163	.01991
50--------------	.01845	.07199	.03239	.02723	.01439	.01033	.01872
55--------------	.01939	.07352	.03314	.02783	.01242	·.00913	.01766
60--------------	.02092	.07533	.03443	.02823	.01005	.00804	.01678
65--------------	.02329	.07684	.03650	.02787	.00753	.00716	.01619
70--------------	.02702	.07780	.03977	.02614	.00521	.00639	.01628
75--------------	.03238	.07744	.04383	.02265	.00363	.00559	.01714
80--------------	:04056	.07641	.04907	.01788	.00252	.00454	.01892
85--------------	.05109	.07742	.05610	.01331	.00168	.00333	.02144

Table 13. PROBABILITY OF EVENTUALLY DYING FROM SPECIFIED CAUSES FOR WHITE FEMALES: UNITED STATES, 1969-71

Exact age in years	Probability for persons at the indicated exact age of eventually dying from the specified cause							
	Malignant neoplasms	Malignant neoplasms of digestive organs	Malignant neoplasms of respiratory system	Diabetes	Diseases of the heart	Ischemic heart disease	Acute myocardial infarction	Cerebro-vascular diseases
0---------------	0.15924	0.05028	0.01333	0.02444	0.42108	0.38194	0.16486	0.15090
1---------------	.16167	.05106	.01354	.02481	.42754	.38788	.16743	.15321
5---------------	.16183	.05119	.01357	.02487	.42865	.38893	.16788	.15360
10--------------	.16179	.05127	.01359	.02491	.42931	.38956	.16815	.15382
15--------------	.16179	.05134	.01361	.02492	.42989	.39011	.16839	.15401
20--------------	.16199	.05148	.01364	.02497	.43107	.39124	.16887	.15441
25--------------	.16218	.05163	.01368	.02501	.43237	.39250	.16941	.15482
30--------------	.16221	.05177	.01372	.02502	.43377	.39388	.16999	.15526
35--------------	.16191	.05190	.01373	.02503	.43553	.39564	.17072	.15577
40--------------	.16099	.05204	.01365	.02506	.43801	.39814	.17168	.15648
45--------------	.15883	.05209	.01340	.02517	.44156	.40174	.17293	.15762
50--------------	.15472	.05200	.01280	.02530	.44655	.40686	.17449	.15935
55--------------	.14828	.05144	.01178	.02541	.45298	.41346	.17613	.16196
60--------------	.13923	.05017	.01039	.02538	.46044	.42123	.17709	.16585
65--------------	.12831	.04818	.00889	.02496	.46785	.42907	.17618	.17108
70--------------	.11511	.04497	.00735	.02385	.47500	.43645	.17214	.17785
75--------------	.10068	.04071	.00594	.02179	.48080	.44204	.16366	.18522
80--------------	.08385	.03497	.00458	.01841	.48650	.44708	.15083	.19231
85--------------	.06694	.02808	.00346	.01410	.49121	.45074	.13527	.19555

Table 13. PROBABILITY OF EVENTUALLY DYING FROM SPECIFIED CAUSES FOR WHITE FEMALES: UNITED STATES, 1969-71—Con.

Exact age in years	Probability for persons at the indicated exact age of eventually dying from the specified cause—Con.						
	Arterio-sclerosis	Diseases of respiratory system	Influenza and pneumonia	Bronchitis, emphysema, and asthma	Cirrhosis of liver	Motor vehicle accidents	All other accidents
0---------------	0.03045	0.04831	0.03500	0.00730	0.00905	0.01185	0.02143
1---------------	.03093	.04767	.03441	.00739	.00918	.01193	.02138
5---------------	.03101	.04746	.03428	.00739	.00920	.01157	.02090
10--------------	.03106	.04742	.03425	.00739	.00920	.01121	.02068
15--------------	.03110	.04739	.03423	.00739	.00921	.01089	.02050
20--------------	.03119	.04740	.03424	.00740	.00922	.00968	.02029
25--------------	.03130	.04741	.03427	.00740	.00923	.00869	.02009
30--------------	.03141	.04740	.03427	.00740	.00921	.00803	.01989
35--------------	.03156	.04739	.03430	.00740	.00913	.00746	.01966
40--------------	.03179	.04740	.03434	.00739	.00885	.00690	.01944
45--------------	.03216	.04743	.03445	.00736	.00825	.00635	.01922
50--------------	.03273	.04750	.03469	.00726	.00733	.00582	.01902
55--------------	.03361	.04757	.03505	.00707	.00615	.00524	.01887
60--------------	.03491	.04769	.03568	.00671	.00489	.00466	.01886
65--------------	.03681	.04799	.03669	.00621	.00373	.00408	.01905
70--------------	.03970	.04874	.03831	.00559	.00273	.00342	.01962
75--------------	.04411	.05036	.04086	.00491	.00198	.00262	.02067
80--------------	.05115	.05336	.04476	.00426	.00134	.00176	.02220
85--------------	.06149	.05853	.05054	.00377	.00082	.00101	.02382

Table 14. PROBABILITY OF EVENTUALLY DYING FROM SPECIFIED CAUSES FOR MALES OTHER THAN WHITE: UNITED STATES, 1969-71

Exact age in years	Probability for persons at the indicated exact age of eventually dying from the specified cause							
	Malignant neoplasms	Malignant neoplasms of digestive organs	Malignant neoplasms of respiratory system	Diabetes	Diseases of the heart	Ischemic heart disease	Acute myocardial infarction	Cerebro-vascular diseases
0---------------	0.15352	0.04736	0.04368	0.01675	0.31723	0.27035	0.12157	0.10619
1---------------	.15890	.04902	.04521	.01733	.32816	.27988	.12585	.10985
5---------------	.15959	.04930	.04547	.01743	.32991	.28149	.12657	.11042
10--------------	.15984	.04946	.04563	.01749	.33095	.28243	.12700	.11076
15--------------	.16015	.04963	.04578	.01753	.33200	.28340	.12743	.11109
20--------------	.16160	.05018	.04630	.01771	.33559	.28664	.12888	.11226
25--------------	.16466	.05120	.04730	.01803	.34235	.29276	.13160	.11452
30--------------	.16796	.05230	.04839	.01826	.34936	.29924	.13442	.11683
35--------------	.17161	.05348	.04959	.01850	.35672	.30619	.13730	.11929
40--------------	.17577	.05494	.05071	.01859	.36448	.31387	.14031	.12214
45--------------	.17953	.05634	.05123	.01873	.37217	.32157	.14264	.12536
50--------------	.18160	.05722	.05052	.01896	.37952	.32905	.14434	.12930
55--------------	.18067	.05741	.04779	.01891	.38682	.33643	.14484	.13397
60--------------	.17591	.05617	.04312	.01888	.39394	.34391	.14461	.13935
65--------------	.16797	.05364	.03736	.01824	.40093	.35101	.14301	.14578
70--------------	.15699	.05044	.03042	.01738	.40757	.35789	.14008	.15036
75--------------	.14236	.04542	.02363	.01591	.41449	.36521	.13662	.15538
80--------------	.12407	.03978	.01738	.01351	.42282	.37241	.13268	.15978
85--------------	.10352	.03325	.01274	.01156	.43430	.38197	.13041	.16108

.5-54

Table 14. PROBABILITY OF EVENTUALLY DYING FROM SPECIFIED CAUSES FOR MALES OTHER THAN WHITE: UNITED STATES, 1969-71—Con.

Exact age in years	Probability for persons at the indicated exact age of eventually dying from the specified cause—Con.						
	Arterio-sclerosis	Diseases of respiratory system	Influenza and pneumonia	Bronchitis, emphysema, and asthma	Cirrhosis of liver	Motor vehicle accidents	All other accidents
0--------------	0.01144	0.06341	0.04042	0.01167	0.02055	0.03176	0.04261
1--------------	.01185	.06057	.03766	.01200	.02127	.03277	.04299
5--------------	.01192	.05991	.03714	.01199	.02138	.03227	.04176
10-------------	.01196	.05992	.03715	.01200	.02145	.03139	.04091
15-------------	.01200	.05995	.03718	.01200	.02152	.03086	.03980
20-------------	.01214	.06026	.03740	.01207	.02175	.02890	.03756
25-------------	.01240	.06098	.03786	.01226	.02207	.02510	.03492
30-------------	.01270	.06159	.03821	.01246	.02196	.02204	.03253
35-------------	.01306	.06210	.03844	.01270	.02102	.01935	.03018
40-------------	.01355	.06232	.03845	.01291	.01898	.01709	.02780
45-------------	.01421	.06260	.03844	.01319	.01615	.01500	.02530
50-------------	.01515	.06280	.03842	.01347	.01307	.01302	.02314
55-------------	.01643	.06323	.03880	.01358	.01018	.01117	.02090
60-------------	.01825	.06362	.03972	.01327	.00757	.00935	.01942
65-------------	.02070	.06445	.04118	.01296	.00523	.00774	.01808
70-------------	.02379	.06616	.04363	.01241	.00333	.00638	.01757
75-------------	.02801	.06799	.04667	.01169	.00230	.00542	.01736
80-------------	.03361	.06891	.04966	.01031	.00169	.00412	.01805
85-------------	.03966	.07074	.05288	.00892	.00140	.00280	.01920

Table 15. PROBABILITY OF EVENTUALLY DYING FROM SPECIFIED CAUSES FOR FEMALES OTHER THAN WHITE: UNITED STATES, 1969-71

Exact age in years	Probability for persons at the indicated exact age of eventually dying from the specified cause							
	Malignant neoplasms	Malignant neoplasms of digestive organs	Malignant neoplasms of respiratory system	Diabetes	Diseases of the heart	Ischemic heart disease	Acute myocardial infarction	Cerebro-vascular diseases
0--------------	0.13477	0.04222	0.01107	0.03660	0.37200	0.31777	0.11935	0.15991
1--------------	.13857	.04342	.01138	.03764	.38230	.32680	.12274	.16438
5--------------	.13900	.04362	.01143	.03781	.38401	.32836	.12332	.16513
10-------------	.13910	.04372	.01146	.03789	.38482	.32912	.12361	.16548
15-------------	.13917	.04381	.01148	.03795	.38549	.32978	.12385	.16577
20-------------	.13953	.04399	.01153	.03808	.38698	.33124	.12440	.16643
25-------------	.14013	.04427	.01160	.03827	.38933	.33349	.12522	.16742
30-------------	.14071	.04458	.01169	.03849	.39215	.33634	.12624	.16854
35-------------	.14108	.04498	.01177	.03880	.39589	.34012	.12753	.16986
40-------------	.14079	.04540	.01175	.03916	.40090	.34520	.12919	.17170
45-------------	.13922	.04581	.01147	.03952	.40678	.35134	.13100	.17404
50-------------	.13555	.04599	.01090	.03972	.41397	.35879	.13288	.17677
55-------------	.12964	.04564	.01004	.03932	.42132	.36657	.13428	.18044
60-------------	.12132	.04443	.00892	.03778	.42931	.37511	.13514	.18524
65-------------	.11245	.04281	.00802	.03525	.43637	.38266	.13439	.19015
70-------------	.10188	.04017	.00699	.03175	.44368	.39034	.13233	.19457
75-------------	.08968	.03630	.00557	.02727	.45142	.39817	.13011	.19801
80-------------	.07748	.03136	.00439	.02291	.45823	.40436	.12659	.19875
85-------------	.06563	.02715	.00331	.01800	.46416	.40973	.12102	.19866

Table 15. PROBABILITY OF EVENTUALLY DYING FROM SPECIFIED CAUSES FOR FEMALES OTHER THAN WHITE: UNITED STATES, 1969-71—Con.

Exact age in years	Probability for persons at the indicated exact age of eventually dying from the specified cause—Con.						
	Arterio-sclerosis	Diseases of respiratory system	Influenza and pneumonia	Bronchitis, emphysema, and asthma	Cirrhosis of liver	Motor vehicle accidents	All other accidents
0---------------	0.01995	0.04565	0.03455	0.00483	0.01313	0.01056	0.02158
1---------------	.02052	.04268	.03205	.00490	.01349	.01077	.02120
5---------------	.02061	.04215	.03168	.00486	.01354	.01030	.02016
10--------------	.02066	.04206	.03162	.00485	.01356	.00975	.01967
15--------------	.02070	.04198	.03157	.00483	.01358	.00947	.01931
20--------------	.02080	.04193	.03156	.00480	.01361	.00876	.01888
25--------------	.02094	.04183	.03156	.00475	.01362	.00785	.01840
30--------------	.02113	.04168	.03153	.00467	.01335	.00713	.01792
35--------------	.02141	.04144	.03148	.00459	.01251	.00644	.01750
40--------------	.02184	.04117	.03145	.00446	.01105	.00578	.01702
45--------------	.02246	.04082	.03138	.00430	.00915	.00511	.01670
50--------------	.02336	.04050	.03144	.00406	.00712	.00452	.01643
55--------------	.02461	.04054	.03189	.00380	.00530	.00383	.01630
60--------------	.02630	.04063	.03249	.00350	.00378	.00331	.01652
65--------------	.02865	.04150	.03367	.00325	.00266	.00280	.01683
70--------------	.03182	.04290	.03538	.00304	.00182	.00236	.01725
75--------------	.03547	.04509	.03762	.00293	.00144	.00181	.01807
80--------------	.04027	.04827	.04069	.00275	.00098	.00142	.01879
85--------------	.04563	.05218	.04417	.00253	.00081	.00124	.01909

Table 16. GAIN IN EXPECTATION OF LIFE DUE TO ELIMINATION OF SPECIFIED CAUSES OF DEATH FOR THE
TOTAL POPULATION: UNITED STATES, 1969-71

Exact age in years	Gain in years in expectation of life at the indicated exact age due to elimination of the specified cause							
	Malignant neoplasms	Malignant neoplasms of digestive organs	Malignant neoplasms of respiratory system	Diabetes	Diseases of the heart	Ischemic heart disease	Acute myocardial infarction	Cerebro-vascular diseases
0----------------	2.47	.60	.50	.24	5.86	5.06	2.43	1.19
1----------------	2.52	.61	.51	.25	5.98	5.16	2.48	1.21
5----------------	2.51	.61	.51	.24	5.99	5.17	2.48	1.21
10---------------	2.49	.61	.51	.24	6.00	5.18	2.49	1.20
15---------------	2.48	.62	.51	.24	6.01	5.20	2.49	1.21
20---------------	2.47	.62	.51	.24	6.03	5.22	2.51	1.21
25---------------	2.47	.63	.52	.25	6.07	5.27	2.53	1.22
30---------------	2.45	.62	.52	.24	6.09	5.29	2.54	1.21
35---------------	2.42	.62	.52	.23	6.11	5.31	2.54	1.21
40---------------	2.38	.62	.52	.23	6.10	5.32	2.53	1.21
45---------------	2.29	.61	.50	.23	6.04	5.28	2.49	1.20
50---------------	2.15	.59	.47	.22	5.91	5.18	2.40	1.19
55---------------	1.94	.55	.41	.21	5.71	5.01	2.25	1.17
60---------------	1.68	.50	.34	.20	5.44	4.78	2.05	1.17
65---------------	1.38	.43	.26	.18	5.08	4.47	1.79	1.15
70---------------	1.06	.34	.17	.15	4.64	4.07	1.49	1.11
75---------------	.78	.27	.10	.12	4.15	3.64	1.18	1.05
80---------------	.51	.18	.05	.08	3.62	3.14	.86	.93
85---------------	.31	.12	.03	.05	3.09	2.66	.61	.79

Exact age in years	Gain in years in expectation of life at the indicated exact age due to elimination of the specified cause—Con.						
	Arterio-sclerosis	Diseases of respiratory system	Influenza and pneumonia	Bronchitis, emphysema, and asthma	Cirrhosis of liver	Motor vehicle accidents	All other accidents
0--------------	.13	.83	.47	.20	.28	.70	.63
1--------------	.14	.69	.36	.20	.29	.71	.60
5--------------	.13	.66	.33	.19	.28	.67	.54
10-------------	.13	.65	.33	.19	.28	.64	.51
15-------------	.13	.65	.32	.19	.29	.61	.48
20-------------	.14	.64	.32	.19	.29	.49	.43
25-------------	.14	.64	.32	.20	.29	.36	.38
30-------------	.14	.63	.31	.19	.28	.28	.33
35-------------	.14	.62	.30	.19	.27	.22	.29
40-------------	.14	.61	.30	.19	.25	.18	.26
45-------------	.15	.60	.29	.19	.22	.15	.23
50-------------	.15	.58	.28	.19	.17	.12	.19
55-------------	.15	.55	.26	.18	.13	.09	.16
60-------------	.16	.52	.26	.17	.09	.07	.15
65-------------	.17	.47	.25	.15	.06	.06	.13
70-------------	.17	.41	.23	.11	.03	.03	.11
75-------------	.19	.36	.23	.08	.02	.03	.10
80-------------	.20	.29	.20	.04	.00	.01	.09
85-------------	.21	.25	.20	.03	.01	.01	.09

Table 17. GAIN IN EXPECTATION OF LIFE DUE TO ELIMINATION OF SPECIFIED CAUSES OF DEATH FOR WHITE MALES: UNITED STATES, 1969-71

Exact age in years	Gain in years in expectation of life at the indicated exact age due to elimination of the specified cause							
	Malignant neoplasms	Malignant neoplasms of digestive organs	Malignant neoplasms of respiratory system	Diabetes	Diseases of the heart	Ischemic heart disease	Acute myocardial infarction	Cerebro-vascular diseases
0---------------	2.31	.55	.69	.17	6.14	5.45	3.01	.86
1---------------	2.35	.56	.71	.17	6.26	5.56	3.07	.88
5---------------	2.34	.56	.71	.17	6.28	5.58	3.08	.88
10--------------	2.33	.57	.72	.18	6.30	5.60	3.10	.88
15--------------	2.31	.57	.72	.17	6.30	5.61	3.10	.88
20--------------	2.31	.57	.72	.17	6.35	5.65	3.13	.89
25--------------	2.30	.57	.73	.17	6.40	5.70	3.15	.89
30--------------	2.28	.57	.73	.17	6.43	5.74	3.17	.89
35--------------	2.26	.57	.73	.16	6.45	5.76	3.18	.89
40--------------	2.23	.57	.73	.16	6.42	5.75	3.16	.88
45--------------	2.18	.56	.71	.16	6.32	5.67	3.08	.88
50--------------	2.08	.54	.68	.15	6.11	5.48	2.92	.88
55--------------	1.93	.51	.61	.14	5.79	5.19	2.68	.87
60--------------	1.71	.46	.52	.13	5.37	4.82	2.37	.87
65--------------	1.43	.40	.40	.12	4.88	4.37	2.01	.87
70--------------	1.12	.32	.27	.10	4.32	3.86	1.61	.85
75--------------	.82	.25	.17	.08	3.76	3.34	1.24	.81
80--------------	.54	.17	.08	.06	3.20	2.82	.88	.72
85--------------	.33	.11	.04	.04	2.67	2.32	.61	.60

Table 17. GAIN IN EXPECTATION OF LIFE DUE TO ELIMINATION OF SPECIFIED CAUSES OF DEATH FOR WHITE MALES: UNITED STATES, 1969-71—Con.

Exact age in years	Gain in years in expectation of life at the indicated exact age due to elimination of the specified cause—Con.						
	Arterio-sclerosis	Diseases of respiratory system	Influenza and pneumonia	Bronchitis, emphysema, and asthma	Cirrhosis of liver	Motor vehicle accidents	All other accidents
0--------------	.09	.86	.41	.26	.30	.93	.76
1--------------	.09	.74	.31	.26	.30	.94	.74
5--------------	.10	.72	.30	.26	.30	.91	.68
10-------------	.10	.72	.30	.27	.31	.88	.66
15-------------	.10	.71	.29	.27	.31	.85	.61
20-------------	.10	.71	.29	.27	.31	.67	.54
25-------------	.10	.70	.29	.27	.31	.46	.46
30-------------	.10	.70	.28	.27	.31	.35	.39
35-------------	.10	.69	.28	.27	.30	.27	.33
40-------------	.10	.69	.27	.27	.28	.21	.28
45-------------	.11	.69	.27	.27	.25	.17	.24
50-------------	.11	.67	.26	.27	.21	.13	.20
55-------------	.11	.65	.25	.27	.16	.10	.16
60-------------	.12	.62	.24	.25	.11	.08	.13
65-------------	.13	.58	.23	.23	.07	.06	.11
70-------------	.13	.50	.22	.18	.04	.04	.09
75-------------	.15	.42	.22	.13	.02	.03	.09
80-------------	.15	.33	.20	.08	.01	.02	.07
85-------------	.16	.26	.18	.04	.01	.01	.07

Table 18. GAIN IN EXPECTATION OF LIFE DUE TO ELIMINATION OF SPECIFIED CAUSES OF DEATH FOR WHITE FEMALES: UNITED STATES, 1969-71

Exact age in years	Gain in years in expectation of life at the indicated exact age due to elimination of the specified cause							
	Malignant neoplasms	Malignant neoplasms of digestive organs	Malignant neoplasms of respiratory system	Diabetes	Diseases of the heart	Ischemic heart disease	Acute myocardial infarction	Cerebro-vascular diseases
0---------------	2.57	.62	.22	.28	5.17	4.40	1.79	1.36
1---------------	2.60	.63	.23	.29	5.25	4.47	1.82	1.39
5---------------	2.59	.63	.23	.29	5.26	4.48	1.82	1.39
10--------------	2.58	.64	.23	.29	5.27	4.49	1.83	1.39
15--------------	2.56	.63	.23	.28	5.27	4.49	1.82	1.38
20--------------	2.55	.63	.23	.28	5.28	4.51	1.83	1.39
25--------------	2.54	.63	.23	.28	5.29	4.52	1.84	1.38
30--------------	2.52	.64	.23	.28	5.30	4.54	1.84	1.38
35--------------	2.48	.63	.23	.28	5.31	4.55	1.85	1.38
40--------------	2.41	.62	.22	.27	5.31	4.56	1.84	1.37
45--------------	2.28	.61	.21	.26	5.30	4.57	1.83	1.36
50--------------	2.09	.59	.19	.26	5.29	4.57	1.82	1.35
55--------------	1.84	.55	.16	.26	5.25	4.55	1.78	1.34
60--------------	1.54	.49	.12	.24	5.14	4.48	1.69	1.32
65--------------	1.25	.43	.09	.22	4.95	4.33	1.56	1.30
70--------------	.95	.35	.06	.19	4.66	4.08	1.36	1.26
75--------------	.68	.26	.04	.14	4.24	3.70	1.10	1.18
80--------------	.45	.18	.02	.10	3.73	3.24	.82	1.05
85--------------	.27	.11	.01	.05	3.15	2.71	.57	.86

Table 18. GAIN IN EXPECTATION OF LIFE DUE TO ELIMINATION OF SPECIFIED CAUSES OF DEATH FOR WHITE FEMALES: UNITED STATES, 1969-71—Con.

Exact age in years	Gain in years in expectation of life at the indicated exact age due to elimination of the specified cause—Con.						
	Arterio-sclerosis	Diseases of respiratory system	Influenza and pneumonia	Bronchitis, emphysema, and asthma	Cirrhosis of liver	Motor vehicle accidents	All other accidents
0---------------	.17	.61	.40	.10	.20	.41	.35
1---------------	.18	.52	.32	.11	.20	.41	.33
5---------------	.18	.49	.31	.10	.20	.39	.29
10---------------	.18	.49	.31	.11	.21	.37	.28
15---------------	.17	.48	.29	.10	.20	.34	.25
20---------------	.18	.47	.29	.10	.20	.27	.24
25---------------	.18	.47	.29	.10	.20	.21	.23
30---------------	.18	.46	.28	.10	.20	.18	.22
35---------------	.18	.45	.28	.10	.19	.15	.20
40---------------	.18	.44	.27	.10	.18	.13	.19
45---------------	.18	.42	.26	.09	.15	.10	.17
50---------------	.18	.41	.26	.09	.13	.09	.16
55---------------	.19	.39	.25	.08	.10	.07	.15
60---------------	.19	.36	.24	.07	.06	.05	.13
65---------------	.20	.33	.23	.06	.04	.05	.13
70---------------	.21	.31	.23	.05	.03	.03	.12
75---------------	.21	.27	.21	.03	.01	.02	.11
80---------------	.22	.25	.20	.02	.01	.01	.10
85---------------	.22	.21	.18	.01	.00	.00	.08

Table 19. GAIN IN EXPECTATION OF LIFE DUE TO ELIMINATION OF SPECIFIED CAUSES OF DEATH FOR MALES OTHER THAN WHITE: UNITED STATES, 1969-71

Exact age in years	Gain in years in expectation of life at the indicated exact age due to elimination of the specified cause							
	Malignant neoplasms	Malignant neoplasms of digestive organs	Malignant neoplasms of respiratory system	Diabetes	Diseases of the heart	Ischemic heart disease	Acute myocardial infarction	Cerebro-vascular diseases
0----------------	2.33	.64	.66	.24	5.29	4.17	1.71	1.36
1----------------	2.40	.66	.68	.24	5.46	4.31	1.76	1.40
5----------------	2.40	.66	.68	.24	5.48	4.34	1.77	1.40
10---------------	2.39	.66	.68	.24	5.49	4.35	1.77	1.41
15---------------	2.39	.67	.69	.25	5.51	4.37	1.79	1.41
20---------------	2.40	.68	.70	.26	5.56	4.42	1.81	1.43
25---------------	2.43	.69	.71	.25	5.65	4.51	1.84	1.45
30---------------	2.46	.69	.73	.25	5.73	4.59	1.87	1.46
35---------------	2.49	.71	.74	.25	5.79	4.66	1.89	1.47
40---------------	2.50	.71	.74	.24	5.80	4.69	1.89	1.47
45---------------	2.48	.71	.73	.23	5.74	4.67	1.84	1.46
50---------------	2.38	.68	.67	.21	5.59	4.57	1.76	1.44
55---------------	2.20	.65	.59	.21	5.38	4.41	1.65	1.42
60---------------	1.94	.57	.47	.19	5.10	4.19	1.50	1.37
65---------------	1.66	.49	.37	.17	4.77	3.93	1.33	1.32
70---------------	1.36	.41	.25	.14	4.40	3.62	1.15	1.22
75---------------	1.06	.32	.17	.11	3.98	3.28	.97	1.11
80---------------	.76	.23	.10	.08	3.55	2.91	.80	.98
85---------------	.51	.15	.06	.05	3.18	2.58	.65	.82

Table 19. GAIN IN EXPECTATION OF LIFE DUE TO ELIMINATION OF SPECIFIED CAUSES OF DEATH FOR MALES OTHER THAN WHITE: UNITED STATES, 1969-71—Con.

Exact age in years	Gain in years in expectation of life at the indicated exact age due to elimination of the specified cause—Con.						
	Arterio-sclerosis	Diseases of respiratory system	Influenza and pneumonia	Bronchitis, emphysema, and asthma	Cirrhosis of liver	Motor vehicle accidents	All other accidents
0--------------	.09	1.22	.81	.17	.46	.97	1.21
1--------------	.09	.94	.57	.17	.47	.99	1.18
5--------------	.09	.88	.53	.16	.47	.96	1.09
10-------------	.09	.87	.53	.16	.47	.90	1.04
15-------------	.10	.87	.53	.17	.48	.88	.98
20-------------	.10	.87	.53	.17	.49	.78	.87
25-------------	.10	.86	.52	.16	.49	.61	.73
30-------------	.10	.84	.51	.16	.47	.48	.62
35-------------	.11	.82	.49	.16	.43	.38	.53
40-------------	.11	.79	.47	.16	.36	.30	.44
45-------------	.11	.75	.44	.16	.28	.23	.36
50-------------	.11	.70	.40	.15	.19	.18	.29
55-------------	.13	.65	.38	.15	.14	.14	.23
60-------------	.13	.60	.35	.13	.09	.10	.19
65-------------	.15	.55	.33	.12	.06	.08	.16
70-------------	.16	.50	.32	.10	.03	.05	.13
75-------------	.17	.45	.30	.08	.02	.04	.11
80-------------	.17	.39	.27	.06	.01	.03	.10
85-------------	.17	.33	.24	.04	.00	.01	.08

Table 20. GAIN IN EXPECTATION OF LIFE DUE TO ELIMINATION OF SPECIFIED CAUSES OF DEATH FOR FEMALES OTHER THAN WHITE: UNITED STATES, 1969-71

Exact age in years	Gain in years in expectation of life at the indicated exact age due to elimination of the specified cause							
	Malignant neoplasms	Malignant neoplasms of digestive organs	Malignant neoplasms of respiratory system	Diabetes	Diseases of the heart	Ischemic heart disease	Acute myocardial infarction	Cerebro-vascular diseases
0----------------	2.41	.61	.20	.55	6.28	4.89	1.62	2.16
1----------------	2.47	.63	.20	.57	6.43	5.03	1.67	2.21
5----------------	2.46	.63	.20	.57	6.45	5.05	1.67	2.22
10---------------	2.46	.63	.20	.57	6.46	5.06	1.68	2.22
15---------------	2.46	.64	.21	.58	6.47	5.08	1.69	2.23
20---------------	2.45	.64	.20	.57	6.48	5.09	1.69	2.23
25---------------	2.45	.64	.21	.58	6.51	5.13	1.70	2.24
30---------------	2.43	.64	.20	.57	6.53	5.16	1.71	2.24
35---------------	2.40	.65	.21	.58	6.55	5.20	1.72	2.23
40---------------	2.33	.64	.20	.57	6.55	5.23	1.72	2.21
45---------------	2.21	.63	.19	.56	6.51	5.23	1.70	2.19
50---------------	2.01	.60	.16	.54	6.44	5.20	1.66	2.13
55---------------	1.76	.56	.14	.50	6.29	5.11	1.59	2.08
60---------------	1.49	.50	.11	.44	6.09	4.97	1.50	2.02
65---------------	1.23	.44	.09	.37	5.78	4.74	1.35	1.93
70---------------	.97	.36	.06	.29	5.41	4.44	1.19	1.80
75---------------	.73	.28	.05	.22	4.98	4.08	1.02	1.62
80---------------	.52	.20	.03	.15	4.50	3.67	.85	1.41
85---------------	.36	.14	.01	.09	4.06	3.28	.68	1.21

Table 20. GAIN IN EXPECTATION OF LIFE DUE TO ELIMINATION OF SPECIFIED CAUSES OF DEATH FOR FEMALES OTHER THAN WHITE: UNITED STATES, 1969-71—Con.

Exact age in years	Gain in years in expectation of life at the indicated exact age due to elimination of the specified cause—Con.						
	Arterio-sclerosis	Diseases of respiratory system	Influenza and pneumonia	Bronchitis, emphysema, and asthma	Cirrhosis of liver	Motor vehicle accidents	All other accidents
0---------------	.16	.96	.70	.10	.35	.37	.54
1---------------	.17	.68	.47	.10	.36	.38	.48
5---------------	.16	.63	.43	.09	.36	.34	.40
10---------------	.16	.62	.43	.09	.36	.30	.37
15---------------	.17	.62	.43	.10	.37	.29	.35
20---------------	.17	.61	.42	.09	.36	.25	.32
25---------------	.18	.60	.41	.09	.37	.21	.30
30---------------	.17	.57	.40	.08	.35	.17	.27
35---------------	.18	.55	.39	.08	.31	.14	.25
40---------------	.18	.52	.37	08	.26	.12	.22
45---------------	.19	.49	.35	.07	.20	.10	.20
50---------------	.19	.45	.33	.06	.13	.07	.18
55---------------	.20	.41	.31	.05	.09	.05	.17
60---------------	.21	.38	.29	.04	.05	.04	.16
65---------------	.21	.35	.28	.03	.03	.03	.14
70---------------	.22	.33	.26	.02	.01	.02	.13
75---------------	.23	.31	.25	.02	.01	.02	.13
80---------------	.23	.29	.24	.02	.01	.01	.11
85---------------	.23	.27	.22	.01	.00	.00	.10

5-67

☆ U. S. GOVERNMENT PRINTING OFFICE : 1977 O - 575-961

FILE

DHEW Publication No. (HRA) 75-1150

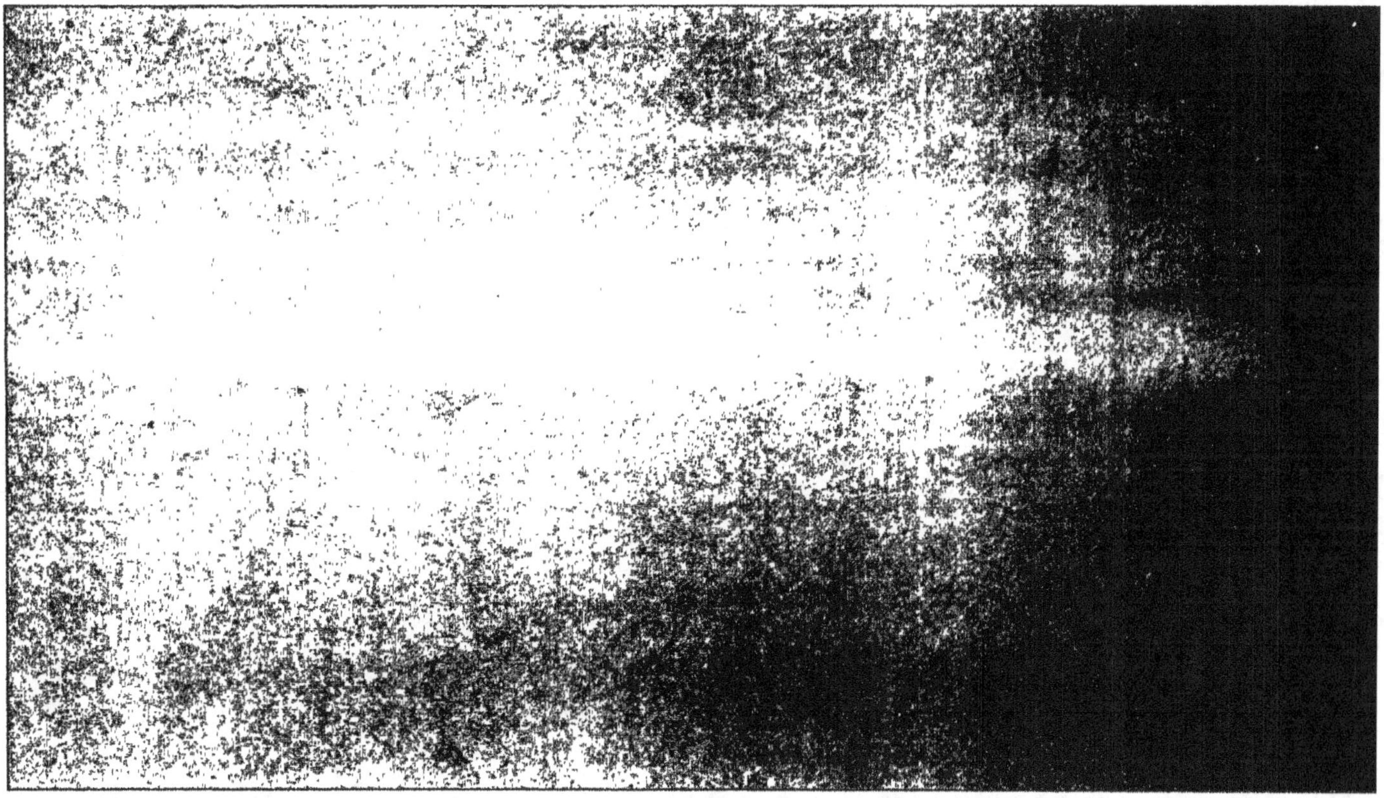

U.S. DEPARTMENT OF HEALTH, EDUCATION, AND WELFARE
PUBLIC HEALTH SERVICE
Health Resources Administration
National Center for Health Statistics
5600 Fishers Lane
Rockville, Maryland 20852

OFFICIAL BUSINESS
Penalty for Private Use $300

www.ingramcontent.com/pod-product-compliance
Lightning Source LLC
Chambersburg PA
CBHW081142290526
45795CB00006B/2341